MARTIN PETERS

A GRAPHIC NOVEL

BY

PATRICK ALLABY

Martin Peters
© 2019 Patrick Allaby

Printed at Gauvin Press, Gatineau, Quebec
First Edition

ISBN 9781772620382
CIP available from Library and Archives Canada

Conundrum Press
Wolfville, NS, Canada
www.conundrumpress.com

This is a work of fiction. Any resemblance to any of the characters portrayed is purely coincidental.

Conundrum Press acknowledges the financial assistance of the Canada Council for the Arts, the Government of Canada, and the Nova Scotia Creative Industries Fund toward this publication.

Canada Council   Conseil des Arts
for the Arts   du Canada

FOR LAURA

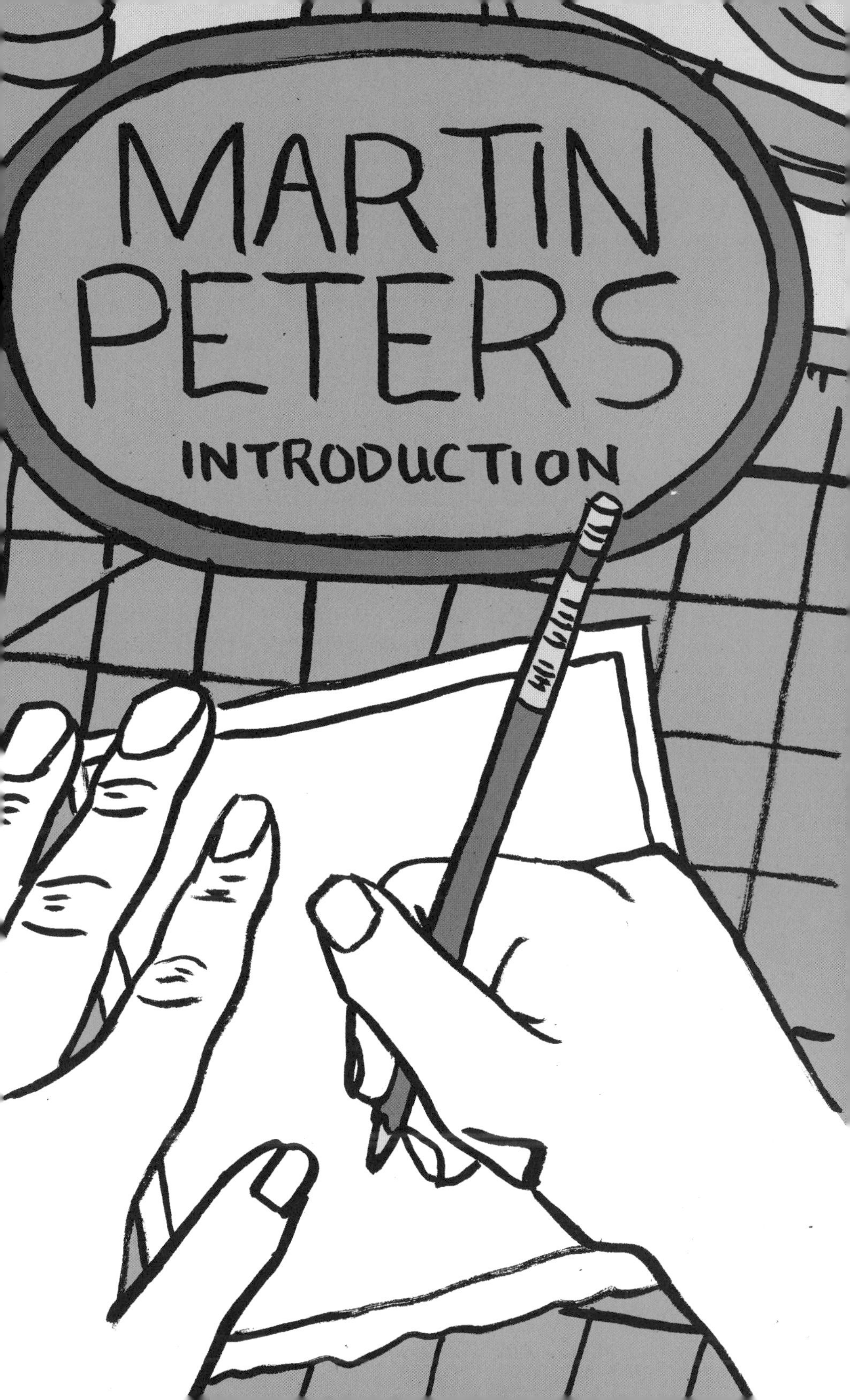
MARTIN
PETERS
INTRODUCTION

I REALIZE THAT, SINCE I'VE CALLED THIS BOOK MARTIN PETERS, YOU MIGHT BE EXPECTING TO FIND A STORY ABOUT A CHARACTER WITH THAT NAME IN THESE PAGES.

AND, WHILE I ASSURE YOU IT'S COMING, I WANTED TO TELL YOU A LITTLE ABOUT MYSELF FIRST.

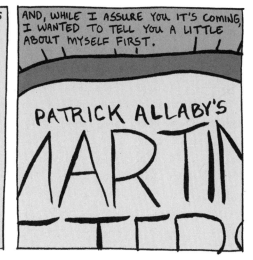

PATRICK ALLABY'S
MARTIN
PETERS

MARTIN PETERS IS BOTH MY FIRST BOOK PUBLISHED BY SOMEONE OTHER THAN MYSELF, AND MY FIRST PRINT RUN OVER FIFTY, SO I GET THE SENSE THAT NOT EVERYONE READING THIS WILL KNOW WHO I AM.

IF I COULD, I WOULD STAND BESIDE EVERY GRAPHIC NOVEL SECTION STOCKING THIS BOOK SO I COULD TELL EVERY POTENTIAL CUSTOMER ITS BACKSTORY,

HI. ARE YOU THINKING OF BUYING THAT?

LIKE I HAVE DONE WITH THE FORTY-FIVE PEOPLE WHO BOUGHT THE XEROXED CHAPTERS OF MARTIN PETERS IN SACKVILLE, FREDERICTON, MONTREAL, PETERBOROUGH, KINGSTON, AND TORONTO BETWEEN APRIL 2017 AND MAY 2018.

IF YOU'RE ON THE FENCE, LET ME TELL YOU A LITTLE ABOUT HOW IT ALL STARTED —

BUT, I JUST DON'T HAVE TIME FOR THAT, SO THIS INTRODUCTION WILL HAVE TO DO.

MARTIN PETERS

So, how did I first meet Martin Peters? Well, it all started in the fall of 2015.

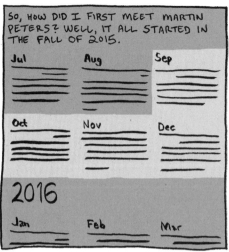

Jul

Aug

Sep

Oct

Nov

Dec

2016

Jan

Feb

Mar

I had just graduated from my BFA and was taking English classes until I figured out what to do with my life, or ran out of money.

During this time, I developed a love of water, and started peeing a lot.

One day, I just realized that water tasted so good.

All my life, water had been this anonymous, tasteless liquid, but suddenly it became this exquisite beverage I couldn't get enough of. I was drinking so much!

I took this trip with my friends to Montreal from Sackville for Expozine in November and bought an 8-pack of 750-ml bottles of water for the drive, so we'd stay hydrated,

1030km

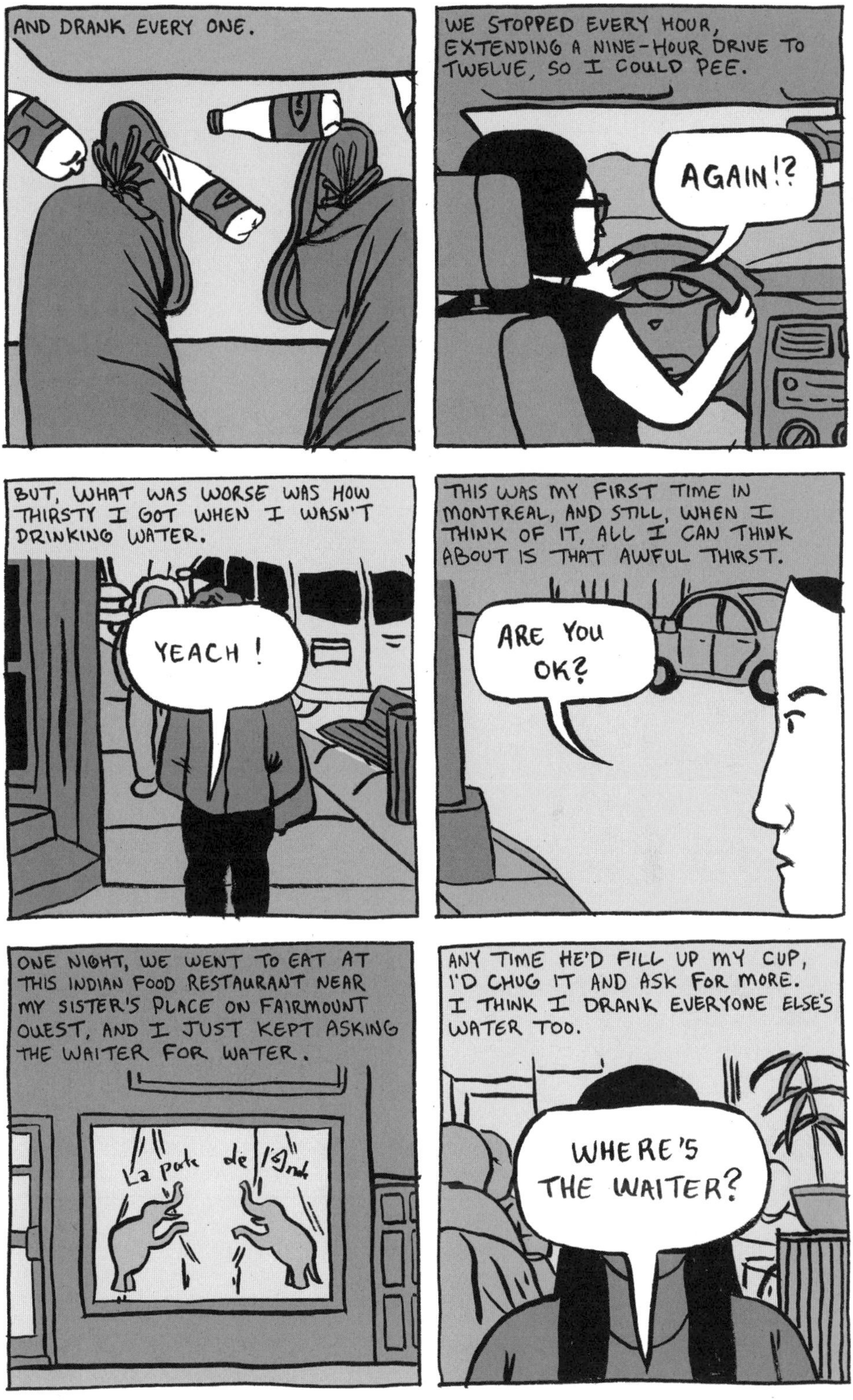
AND DRANK EVERY ONE.
WE STOPPED EVERY HOUR, EXTENDING A NINE-HOUR DRIVE TO TWELVE, SO I COULD PEE.
AGAIN!?
BUT, WHAT WAS WORSE WAS HOW THIRSTY I GOT WHEN I WASN'T DRINKING WATER.
YEACH!
THIS WAS MY FIRST TIME IN MONTREAL, AND STILL, WHEN I THINK OF IT, ALL I CAN THINK ABOUT IS THAT AWFUL THIRST.
ARE YOU OK?
ONE NIGHT, WE WENT TO EAT AT THIS INDIAN FOOD RESTAURANT NEAR MY SISTER'S PLACE ON FAIRMOUNT OUEST, AND I JUST KEPT ASKING THE WAITER FOR WATER.
ANY TIME HE'D FILL UP MY CUP, I'D CHUG IT AND ASK FOR MORE. I THINK I DRANK EVERYONE ELSE'S WATER TOO.
WHERE'S THE WAITER?

IF YOU'VE NEVER EXPERIENCED THE KIND OF THIRST I FELT IN MONTREAL, THERE'S NO WAY I CAN DESCRIBE IT TO YOU. NO CLICHÉ WOULD DO IT JUSTICE.

AS FOR EXPOZINE, THINGS DID NOT GO WELL.

I MADE TWENTY DOLLARS ON THE FIRST DAY AND TWELVE ON THE SECOND,

AND I SPENT THE WHOLE TIME GOING TO THE CANTEEN FOR WATER.

A FRIEND OF MINE TOOK A PHOTO OF ME. IT'S THE SKINNIEST I'VE EVER BEEN.

I SPENT MOST OF THE DRIVE BACK SLEEPING,

AND WHEN I WAS ASKED TO DRIVE FOR AN HOUR BEFORE WE STOPPED IN FREDERICTON FOR SUPPER, I STARTED FALLING ASLEEP AT THE WHEEL.

A WEEK AFTER GETTING HOME FROM EXPOZINE, I WOKE UP AND SPENT THE WHOLE DAY VOMITING.

AT 2AM, I WENT TO THE HOSPITAL WHERE I WAS TOLD I HAD TYPE 1, THEN TYPE 2, AND THEN TYPE 1 DIABETES, AT WHICH POINT I PASSED OUT.

I SPENT MOST OF THE FOLLOWING WEEK IN INTENSIVE CARE,

AND THEN SPENT UNTIL THE END OF JANUARY FINISHING THE FALL SEMESTER.

AT WHICH POINT, I HAD BURNED THROUGH MY SAVINGS, AND THEN SOME, TRYING TO AFFORD INSULIN AND OTHER DIABETIC SUPPLIES.

I FOUGHT WITH THE NEW BRUNSWICK DRUG PLAN FOR MONTHS, TRYING TO GET THEM TO SUBSIDIZE MY LIFE-SUSTAINING MEDICATION. IT TURNED THE TRAUMA OF MY DIAGNOSIS INTO A NEVER-ENDING NIGHTMARE.

I WAS PERSUADED BY A DIABETES EDUCATOR TO JOIN A DIABETIC SUPPORT GROUP TO HELP ME THROUGH THIS ORDEAL.

MAYBE SOMETHING LIKE THAT WOULD BE GOOD FOR YOU...

WHICH IS HOW I MET MARTIN (ALTHOUGH I HAVE TO SAY THAT THE SUPPORT GROUP WAS OTHERWISE TOTALLY USELESS),

AND THE FIVE-THOUSAND DOLLAR GRANT I GOT FROM ARTSNB TO TELL HIS STORY PAID FOR MY INSULIN FOR A FEW MONTHS.

I'D LIKE TO THANK ARTSNB FOR THAT.

I'D ALSO—DESPITE THE WAY THINGS TURNED OUT— LIKE TO THANK MARTIN. I NEVER WOULD HAVE FIGURED OUT HOW TO LIVE WITH DIABETES WITHOUT HIM.

ON A HOUSEKEEPING NOTE, THE THREE CHAPTERS OF MARTIN PETERS WERE DRAWN IN SACKVILLE, NEW BRUNSWICK, BETWEEN SEPTEMBER 2016 AND AUGUST 2017, WHEN I MOVED TO KITCHENER FOR MY MFA.

SO YEAH. THAT'S ABOUT IT.

I SIGNED A CONTRACT WITH CONUNDRUM IN THE FALL OF 2018, AT THE START OF MY SECOND YEAR.

I MEAN THERE'S STILL THE ACTUAL BOOK.

AND ADDED GREY TONES THAT DECEMBER WHEN I WAS HOME FOR CHRISTMAS. I USED PHOTOSHOP FOR THIS.

I REDREW SOME PANELS OVER READING WEEK IN FEBRUARY 2019.

WHAT DO YOU THINK? AM I TALKING TOO MUCH?

FINAL EDITS AND THIS INTRODUCTION WERE DONE IN KITCHENER AND FREDERICTON IN LATE APRIL AND EARLY MAY, AFTER I DEFENDED MY THESIS.

IF YOU WANT TO READ THE BOOK NOW, I'LL SHUT UP AND LEAVE YOU BE. IS THAT OK?

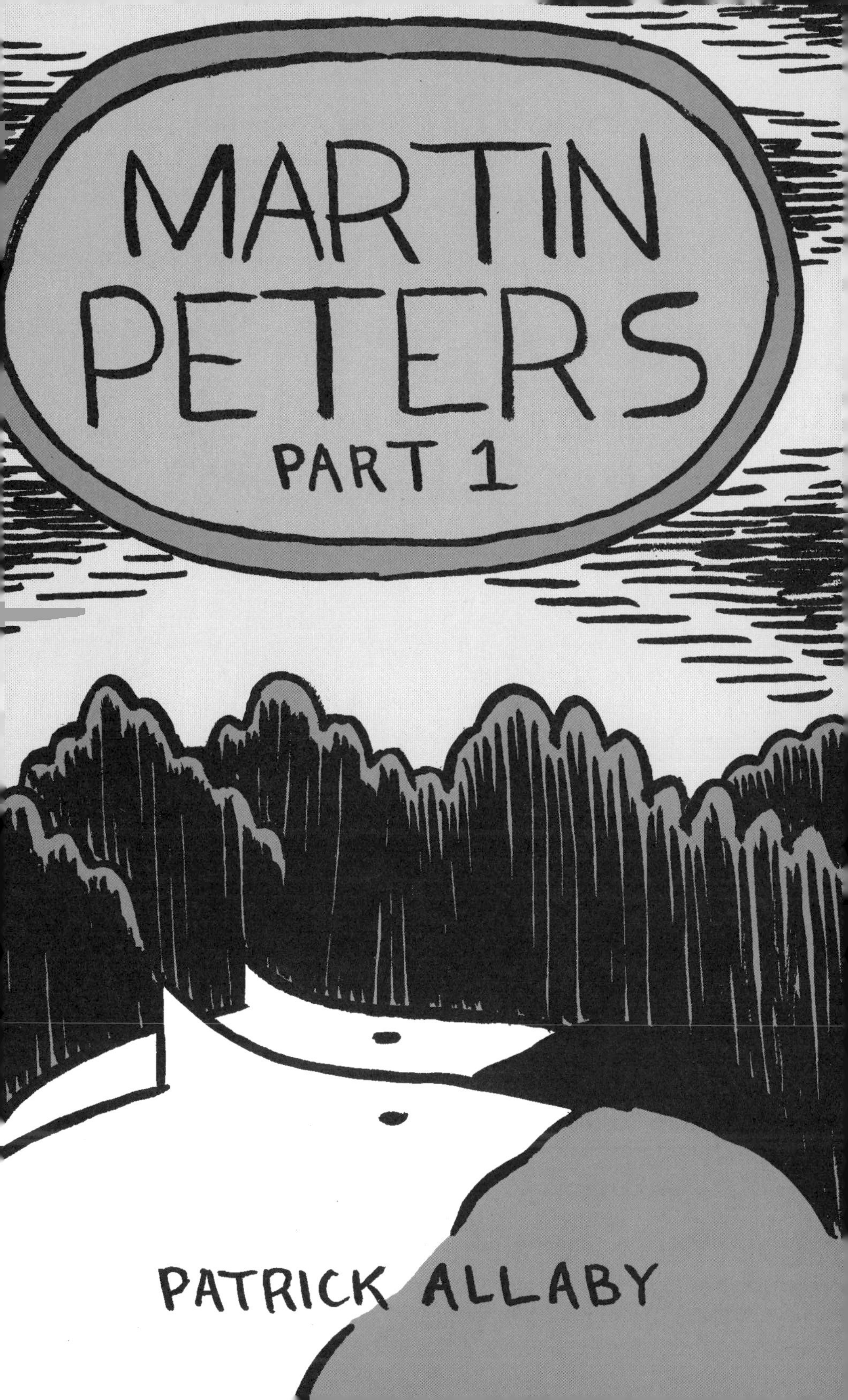
MARTIN PETERS
PART 1
PATRICK ALLABY

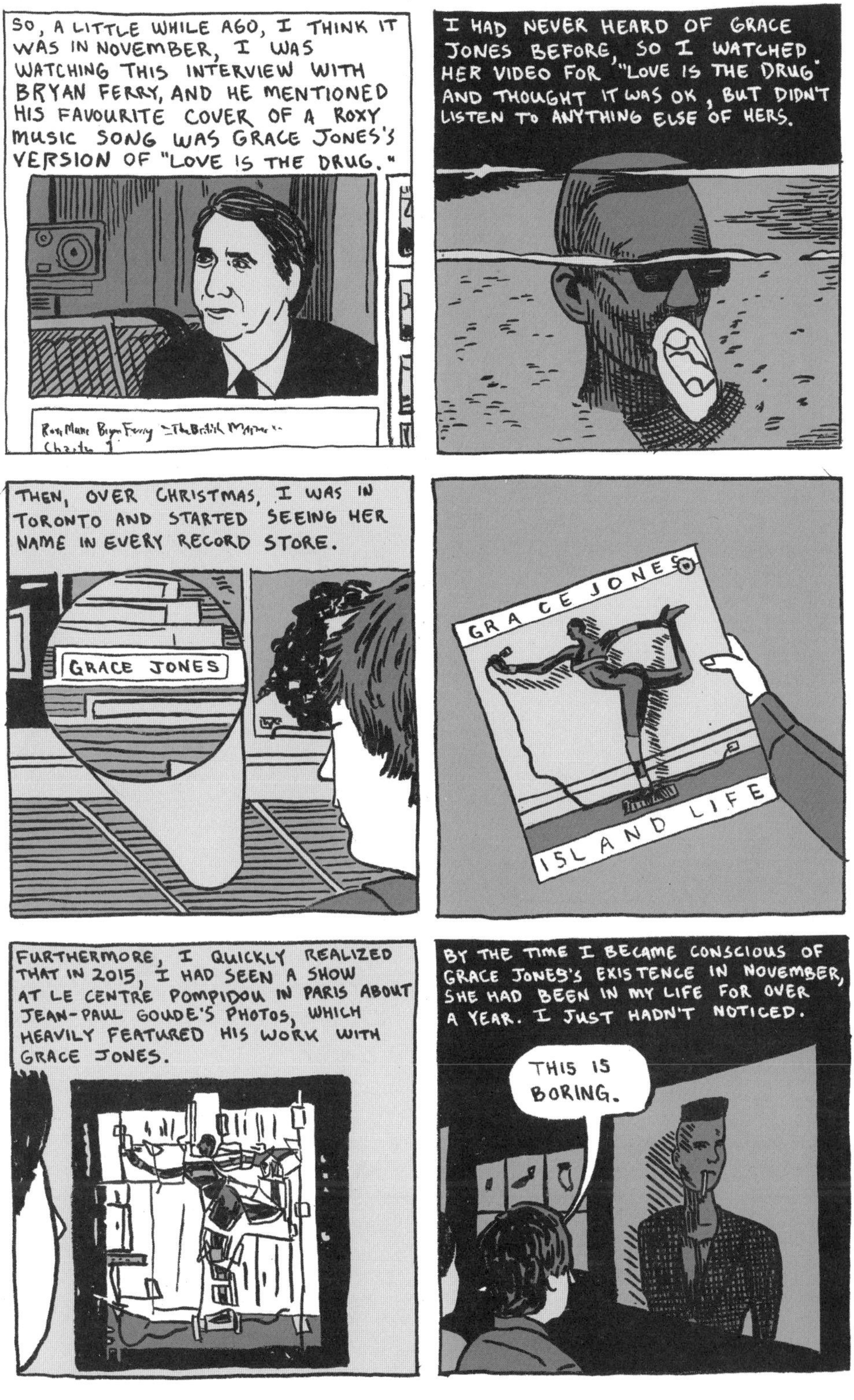

SO, A LITTLE WHILE AGO, I THINK IT WAS IN NOVEMBER, I WAS WATCHING THIS INTERVIEW WITH BRYAN FERRY, AND HE MENTIONED HIS FAVOURITE COVER OF A ROXY MUSIC SONG WAS GRACE JONES'S VERSION OF "LOVE IS THE DRUG."
I HAD NEVER HEARD OF GRACE JONES BEFORE, SO I WATCHED HER VIDEO FOR "LOVE IS THE DRUG" AND THOUGHT IT WAS OK, BUT DIDN'T LISTEN TO ANYTHING ELSE OF HERS.
THEN, OVER CHRISTMAS, I WAS IN TORONTO AND STARTED SEEING HER NAME IN EVERY RECORD STORE.
GRACE JONES
GRACE JONES
ISLAND LIFE
FURTHERMORE, I QUICKLY REALIZED THAT IN 2015, I HAD SEEN A SHOW AT LE CENTRE POMPIDOU IN PARIS ABOUT JEAN-PAUL GOUDE'S PHOTOS, WHICH HEAVILY FEATURED HIS WORK WITH GRACE JONES.
BY THE TIME I BECAME CONSCIOUS OF GRACE JONES'S EXISTENCE IN NOVEMBER, SHE HAD BEEN IN MY LIFE FOR OVER A YEAR. I JUST HADN'T NOTICED.
THIS IS BORING.

SOMETIMES I THINK ABOUT HOW MANY GRACE JONES'S I PASS BY EACH DAY

AND HOW IF I STOPPED AND TRIED TO PAY ATTENTION TO EACH AND EVERY GRACE JONES IN MY LIFE, I'D NEVER—

SINCE THAT TASK IS INCONCEIVABLY LARGE, I'VE PICKED OUT JUST ONE GRACE JONES, NAMED MARTIN PETERS, TO EXPLORE FOR NOW.

I MET MARTIN IN A DIABETES SUPPORT GROUP THAT I STARTED GOING TO IN MONCTON AFTER I WAS DIAGNOSED WITH TYPE 1 IN DECEMBER OF 2015.

HI.

MARTIN AND I ARE ABOUT THE SAME AGE AND WE SOON GOT TO KNOW EACH OTHER.

I WAS DIAGNOSED WHEN I WAS THREE.

IT TURNED OUT THAT WE BOTH GREW UP IN THE SAME FREDERICTON NEIGHBOURHOOD, WENT TO THE SAME SCHOOLS, RODE ON THE SAME BUS, YET HAD SOMEHOW NEVER MET UNTIL THEN. I'D LIKE TO EXTEND MY DEEPEST GRATITUDE TO MARTIN FOR LETTING ME TELL THIS, HIS STORY.

AROUND FREDERICTON HIGH SCHOOL, MARTIN WAS KNOWN FOR TWO THINGS: HAVING DIABETES...

eww!

AND BEING THAT PINK FLOYD KID.

S-SORRY!

HE HAD TWO PINK FLOYD SHIRTS THAT HE WORE ENDLESSLY, AND BY THE FALL OF 2008, WHEN HE WAS IN GRADE 10 (AND WHERE OUR STORY STARTS) HAD ALL BUT ONE OF THEIR ALBUMS.

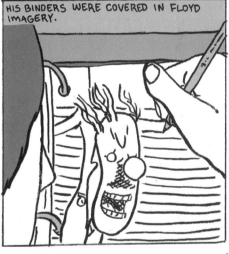
HIS BINDERS WERE COVERED IN FLOYD IMAGERY.

AND HIS FRIENDS ALWAYS SAID THAT HE WOULD GROW UP TO BE A REAL-LIFE FORTY-YEAR-OLD VIRGIN.

IT WOULD HAVE BOTHERED HIM IF HE'D EVER KNOWN ANYTHING ELSE.

COMING FROM A FAMILY WITH A HISTORY OF DIABETES, MARTIN WAS ACUTELY AWARE OF THE DISEASE'S POTENTIAL (OR, MORE REALISTICALLY, PROBABLE) COMPLICATIONS.

CAN I GET YOU ANYTHING, MARTIN?

HE HAD NEVER KNOWN HIS PATERNAL GRANDFATHER TO HAVE TWO FEET

AND, BY THE TIME HE WAS TEN, GRANDPA PETERS WAS ALSO BLIND.

YET, HE STILL WATCHED T.V.

NO "T."

MARTIN'S DAD WOULD TELL HIM ABOUT HOW, IN HIS YOUTH, THEY'D KEEP SUGAR CUBES AROUND THE HOUSE

AND HOW HE'D HAVE TO, EVERY NOW AND THEN, WAKE GRANDPA PETERS BACK UP (THANK GOD FOR BLOOD GLUCOSE METERS!).

DAD?

GRANDPA PETERS DIED TWO DAYS AFTER HIS SIXTY-NINTH BIRTHDAY, ON JANUARY 10, 2009, WHEN MARTIN WAS SIXTEEN.

YOU HAVE TO REMEMBER SCIENCE HAS COME A LONG WAY.

ALTHOUGH TIMES HAD CHANGED IN THE DECADES SINCE MARTIN'S DAD WAS A CHILD, THE MEMORY OF GROWING UP WITH HIS FATHER PERSISTED, AND MARTIN GREW UP HEAVILY SUPERVISED.

ALTHOUGH, IT'S STILL IMPORTANT TO BE CAUTIOUS.

EVEN THOUGH HIS ENDOCRINOLOGIST SAID IT WAS ALRIGHT, MARTIN WASN'T ALLOWED TO ATTEND SLEEP OVERS.

WELL CAN THEY COME OVER HERE?

OR PLAY SPORTS.

HE WAS, HOWEVER, ALLOWED TO GO FOR WALKS.

HOW ARE YOU FEELING?

FINE, DAD.

ALTHOUGH, ON ONE OF HIS LATER, UNSUPERVISED EXPEDITIONS, A POLICE OFFICER ENDED UP DRIVING HIM HOME.

ARE YOU MARTIN?

POLICE

AS A RESULT, MARTIN GREW UP WITH A MORE LIMITED WORLDVIEW THAN OTHER KIDS HIS AGE.

KATHERINE WAS A YEAR YOUNGER THAN MARTIN

AND HAD MOVED TO FREDERICTON FROM A MI'KMAQ COMMUNITY IN NORTHERN NEW BRUNSWICK THAT MARTIN NEVER LEARNT THE NAME OF

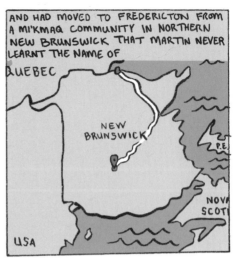

SO HER MOTHER COULD .TAKE NURSING AT U.N.B.

THEY STAYED WHEN SHE WAS HIRED AT THE CHALMERS HOSPITAL.

KATHERINE ALSO LIKED PINK FLOYD, AND MARTIN'S DEVOTION TO THEM STOOD OUT TO HER.

SO, SHE STARTED SITTING BESIDE HIM ON THE BUS AND HOPING HE WOULD NOTICE HER.

FOR SEVERAL WEEKS, SHE SAT BESIDE HIM, AND THEY DIDN'T SPEAK.

IN FACT, SHE WASN'T EVEN SURE HE HAD NOTICED HER.

EVENTUALLY, SHE REALIZED SHE WOULD HAVE TO BE THE ONE TO BREAK THE ICE.

Y'KNOW...

AND GOT UP THE NERVE TO SPEAK FIRST.

MY FAVOURITE FLOYD ALBUM IS THE PIPER AT THE GATES OF DAWN.

YEAH

AT WHICH POINT, THERE WAS NO TURNING BACK.

I THINK IT'S JUST GREAT. SYD WAS A REAL MADCAP IN A WAY NO ONE ELSE IN FLOYD WAS. AS MUCH AS I LOVE ROGER WATERS, [ETC...]

THAT NIGHT, WHEN MARTIN GOT HOME, HE HAD A NEW CONTACT ON M.S.N.

AND UNLIKE MOST NEW CONTACTS, MARTIN SPOKE TO THIS ONE.

hey.

THEY SPOKE UNTIL SUPPER,

MARTIN!

AT WHICH POINT, MARTIN ATE QUICKLY,

DITCHED THE DISHES

MARTIN!

AND HOPPED BACK ON M.S.N. TO FIND OUT SHE WANTED TO MEET UP IN A NEARBY PARK.

back!

do you want to hang out?

MARTIN TOLD HIS PARENTS HE WAS GOING OUT FOR A WALK

HI

BUT SAT AROUND WITH KATHERINE FOR OVER AN HOUR.

IS THAT "NICK AND NORAH'S INFINITE PLAYLIST"?

YAH

OVERHEARD BY ONLY THE OCCASIONAL DOG WALKER, THEY TALKED AND TALKED.

HAVE YOU SEEN THE MOVIE?

MARTIN HAD NEVER HAD SUCH AN ENGAGING CONVERSATION.

I LOVE MICHAEL CERA

HOWEVER, BEFORE TOO LONG, THEY WERE INTERRUPTED BY KATHERINE'S PARENTS

KATHERINE!

AND MARTIN WAS LEFT ALONE TO PROCESS WHAT HE'D JUST EXPERIENCED.

WHEN HE FINALLY RETURNED HOME,

UP HIS LONG, BUMPY DRIVEWAY,

IT WAS LATER THAN HE'D EVER STAYED OUT BEFORE,

I'M HOME!

AND HIS MOTHER—AT HER WITS END—DEMANDED TO KNOW WHERE HE'D BEEN.

WE WERE ABOUT TO GO OUT LOOKING FOR YOU!

UNWILLING TO SPILL THE BEANS ABOUT HIS ROMANTIC ESCAPADE, MARTIN GAVE THE VAGUEST POSSIBLE ANSWER

I WAS JUST OUT FOR A WALK!

AND WENT TO BED.

YOU WERE GONE FOR OVER TWO HOURS!

CR
BIT

IN HIS BASEMENT BEDROOM, MARTIN TRIED TO TALK HIMSELF DOWN,

BUT EVEN AFTER JERKING OFF, MARTIN COULDN'T GET HER OUT OF HIS MIND.

AND SO HE LAY AWAKE PLOTTING THE COURSE OF THEIR RELATIONSHIP,

HOW HOLDING HANDS WOULD START A CHAIN OF EVENTS

THAT WOULD LEAD TO A HANDJOB (OR EVEN HANDJOBS)

AND CULMINATE WITH MARTIN LOSING HIS VIRGINITY BY THE END OF OCTOBER.

MARTIN AND KATHERINE BEGAN HANGING OUT ALMOST NIGHTLY,

HEY

HI

BUT BESIDE WALKING, THEY DIDN'T GET PHYSICAL.

AND DESPITE HAVING TO REPEATEDLY REEVALUATE HIS TIMELINE, MARTIN WAS ENJOYING HIMSELF.

STEP 2

8

14

STEP 3

HE HAD ALWAYS FOUND THE SKY IN SKY-LINE ACRES OPPRESSIVE. THERE WERE SO MANY TREES AND POWERLINES RUNNING ABOVE HIS HEAD THAT HE FELT TRAPPED ON THE SIDEWALK.

BUT WITH KATHERINE,

WHAT ARE YOU DOING?

HE FELT DIFFERENT.

THE TWO WOULD MEET UP IN THE ELEMENTARY SCHOOL PLAYGROUND BY THEIR BUS STOP

AND USUALLY HEAD DOWNHILL TOWARDS KIMBLE,

USUALLY WITH A DETOUR THROUGH A SMALLER PARK IN BETWEEN BEACONSFIELD ST. AND LONDON CT.

LATER ON, THIS WOULD BECOME A FAVOURITE SPOT FOR THEM TO GET HIGH,

BUT IN THOSE DAYS, IT WAS MORE COMMON FOR THEM TO EXPLORE DEVELOPMENTS ON THE EDGE OF SKYLINE.

BEFORE LOOPING BACK TO THE SCHOOL.

EVENTUALLY, THEY BEGAN SPENDING LUNCHES TOGETHER TOO.

HEY.

ALTHOUGH IT WAS MORE LIKE MARTIN WAS SPENDING LUNCH WITH KATHERINE AND HER FRIENDS.

WHO'S THIS?

THE MAIN FORM OF ENTERTAINMENT FOR MARTIN'S FRIENDS WAS MAKING FUN OF HIM.

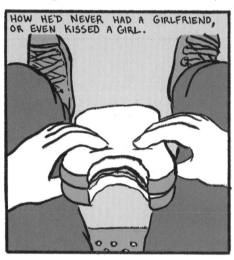

HOW HE'D NEVER HAD A GIRLFRIEND, OR EVEN KISSED A GIRL.

KATHERINE GAVE MARTIN THE PERFECT REASON TO DITCH HIS FRIENDS.

UNFORTUNATELY, EVEN WITH KATHERINE, THEY FOUND A WAY.

SO, I HEAR YOU'RE A CHUBBY CHASER NOW.

UNLIKE MARTIN, KATHERINE WASN'T SURE IF SHE WANTED A RELATIONSHIP.

AND I, LIKE, LIKE DALI, BUT PICASSO IS JUST SO MUCH MORE INTERESTING TO ME...

CERTAINLY, THE IDEA OF STEPPING INTO THE SENSUAL WORLD APPEALED TO HER,

...SSO ...W SO ...T HE ...DRAW ...ILD! ...LL.

BUT SHE ALSO JUST WANTED A FRIEND.

STILL, I LIKE HOW REALISTICALLY DALI DRAWS.

SHE WANTED SOMEONE SHE COULD GO ON WALKS WITH.

AND TALK TO,

I DON'T KNOW... THERE'S SOMETHING I JUST DON'T LIKE ABOUT THE POLICE.

AND MARTIN SEEMED WELL EDUCATED IN HER FAVOURITE TOPICS AND HE WAS AN EXCEPTIONALLY TALENTED WALKER.

WELL, THEY'RE JUST A RADIO-FRIENDLY VERSION OF THE CLASH.

UNLIKE MARTIN, KATHERINE DIDN'T SUFFER FROM A LACK OF REAL FRIENDS.

SO, I WAS LISTENING TO THIS DAVID BOWIE ALBUM, DIAMOND DOGS, WHICH I GOT FOR MY BIRTHDAY AND THE MAIN CHARACTER IS "HALLOWEEN JACK," WHICH IS THE SAME NAME AS THE GUY FROM "NIGHTMARE [...]

ALTHOUGH SHE DID HAVE TROUBLE RELATING TO THE ONES SHE HAD.

MY BROTHER LIKES DAVID [...]

SHE MET JULIA AND GISELE AFTER SHE MOVED TO FREDERICTON THROUGH A BUDDY SYSTEM THAT THE PRINCIPAL OF HER MIDDLE SCHOOL RAN.

JESSICA... I MEAN JULIA.

HI!

HI

THEY HAD VOLUNTEERED TO WELCOME HER TO THE SCHOOL AND SHOW HER AROUND.

IN THE FIVE YEARS SHE'D KNOWN GISELE AND JULIA, KATHERINE HAD NEVER STOPPED FEELING LIKE THE NEW GIRL.

MY BROTHER REALLY LIKES TO BUY MUSIC FROM BACKSTREET RECORDS. IT'S DOWNTOWN BY CITY HALL.

AND SHE LONGED TO BE MORE THAN A RECURRING GUEST ON "LIVE WITH GISELE & JULIA."

ACTUALLY, MY PARENTS GOT ME A GIFT CERTIFICATE FROM THERE FOR MY BIRTHDAY. IT'S WHERE I GOT DIAMOND DOGS.

TO BE FAIR THOUGH, KATHERINE DIDN'T GO ON WALKS WITH MARTIN JUST BECAUSE SHE WANTED A FRIEND.

AS ANYONE WHO GREW UP IN SKYLINE ACRES CAN ATTEST, A BUNGALOW DOESN'T PROVIDE MUCH PRIVACY,

AND IT CAN BE A STRUGGLE TO ESCAPE.

THAT FALL, KATHERINE'S OLDER BROTHER HAD JOINED A RUSH COVER BAND AND PRACTICED DAILY.

RUS 2112

CHRIS!

NOT UNRELATEDLY, HE WAS ALSO FIGHTING CONSTANTLY WITH HIS MOTHER,

WILL
THAT

AND MORE THAN ANYTHING, KATHERINE JUST NEEDED SPACE.

hey

Hi! do you want to go for a walk?

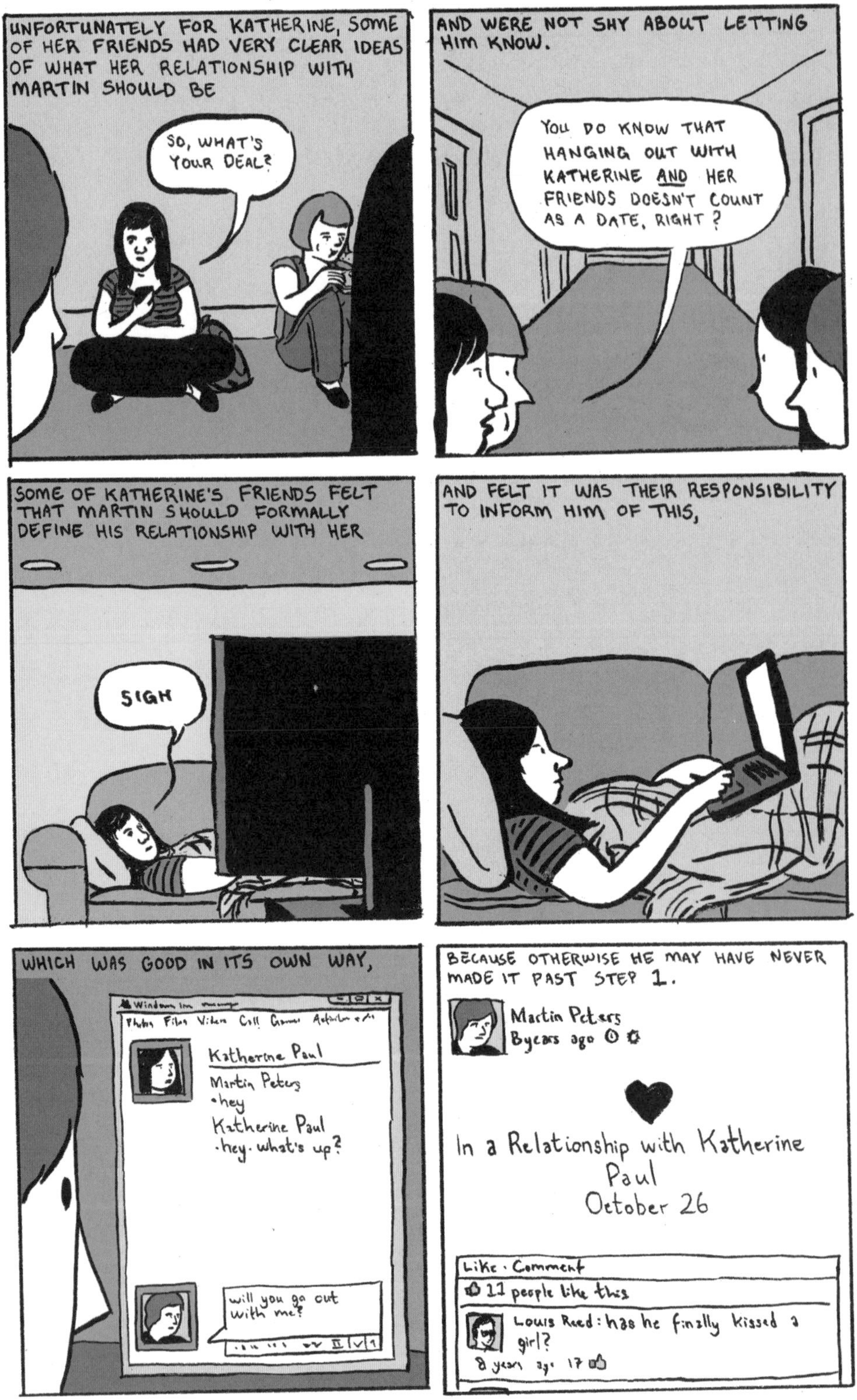
UNFORTUNATELY FOR KATHERINE, SOME OF HER FRIENDS HAD VERY CLEAR IDEAS OF WHAT HER RELATIONSHIP WITH MARTIN SHOULD BE
SO, WHAT'S YOUR DEAL?
AND WERE NOT SHY ABOUT LETTING HIM KNOW.
YOU DO KNOW THAT HANGING OUT WITH KATHERINE AND HER FRIENDS DOESN'T COUNT AS A DATE, RIGHT?
SOME OF KATHERINE'S FRIENDS FELT THAT MARTIN SHOULD FORMALLY DEFINE HIS RELATIONSHIP WITH HER
SIGH
AND FELT IT WAS THEIR RESPONSIBILITY TO INFORM HIM OF THIS,
WHICH WAS GOOD IN ITS OWN WAY,
Katherine Paul
Martin Peters
•hey
Katherine Paul
•hey. what's up?
will you go out with me?
BECAUSE OTHERWISE HE MAY HAVE NEVER MADE IT PAST STEP 1.
Martin Peters
8 years ago
In a Relationship with Katherine Paul
October 26
Like · Comment
11 people like this
Louis Reed: has he finally kissed a girl?
8 years ago 17

IT WAS ON THE FIRST SNOW — SOMETIME IN MID-NOVEMBER—

OH. I THOUGHT MAYBE YOU WERE JEWISH.

THAT MARTIN FINALLY MADE IT TO STEP 2

COME ON. LET'S FIND SHELTER.

HE HAD REVISED HIS PLAN SO MANY TIMES. ITS LATEST ITERATION HAD THEM KISSING AT THE WINTER FORMAL ON DECEMBER 15TH,

DEC·15

YOU ARE HERE

THE LONG DESIRED HANDJOB ON DECEMBER 20TH AND SEX BY 2010.

DEC 20

DEC 31

END

MARTIN WAS SO PROUD OF HIMSELF FOR FINALLY STICKING TO IT,

TALKING ABOUT A MUSICIAN HE HAS NO INTEREST IN.

THAT HE BARELY HEARD A WORD ANYONE SAID TO HIM ALL NIGHT.

THE USUAL CONCERNS ABOUT HOW IF HE GOT LOW BLOOD SUGAR WHILE HE WAS OUT, HE COULD BE IN A LOT OF TROUBLE. THEY NEVER SAY "DIE." THEY ALSO NEVER SEEM TO REMEMBER HIS FAST ACTING SUGAR THAT HE ALWAYS ON HIM.

THE STERN TALKING TO THAT MARTIN RECIEVED FROM HIS PARENTS WAS MORE RELEVANT THAN THEY MIGHT HAVE IMAGINED,

SINCE MARTIN—HOPING TO APPEAR LESS WIMPISH—HAD DECIDED TO HIDE THE FACT HE WAS DIABETIC FROM KATHERINE.

NOT ONLY DO I HAVE SHARP SIGHT, BUT ALSO MY PANCREAS IS IN TOP SHAPE!

ANYTIME HE'D START TO GO LOW — WHICH HAPPENED NOT IRREGULARLY WHILE GETTING EXERCISE—

HE'D TELL HER HE HAD TO TAKE A PISS AND GO TEST HIS BLOOD SUGAR,

DON'T LOOK!

BEEP

IT WAS UNFORTUNATE, BOTH BECAUSE IT LOOKED DISGUSTING TO HER WHEN HE CAME BACK EATING A GRANOLA BAR,

OK, GOO

AND BECAUSE IF ANYTHING EVER HAPPENED, SHE WOULD HAVE NO CLUE WHAT TO DO.

MARTIN

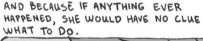

THE SECOND SNOW OF THE SEASON CAME IN THE EARLY HOURS OF THURSDAY, NOVEMBER 27TH.

ON THAT MORNING, MARTIN FOUND HIMSELF ALONE AT THE BUS STOP.

HE WONDERED IF MAYBE KATHERINE HAD WALKED TO SCHOOL WITHOUT TELLING HIM.

OW

BUT, AFTER SEARCHING FOR HER OVER THE LUNCH BREAK, HE GUESSED MAYBE SHE WAS HOME SICK. IF ONLY HE HAD A CELL PHONE.

HOPEFULLY SHE WAS OK.

HOPEFULLY SHE KNEW HE WAS THERE FOR HER.

ONLY AFTER SCHOOL ON FRIDAY DID HE FIND OUT KATHERINE WAS OK AND NOT IN FACT DYING

AND HAD GONE NORTH FOR THE WEEKEND WITHOUT TELLING HIM.

THERE WAS SOME SORT OF FAMILY FUNCTION, AND SHE COULDN'T TALK FOR LONG.

ON TOP OF THAT, KATHERINE'S COUSIN WAS ON THE COMPUTER WITH HER,

AND, WHILE MARTIN WAS HOPING TO DISCUSS RADIO K.A.O.S., ROGER WATERS'S SECOND ALBUM,

HE SPENT THE ENTIRE TIME ANSWERING QUESTIONS ABOUT HIS INTENTIONS WITH KATHERINE.

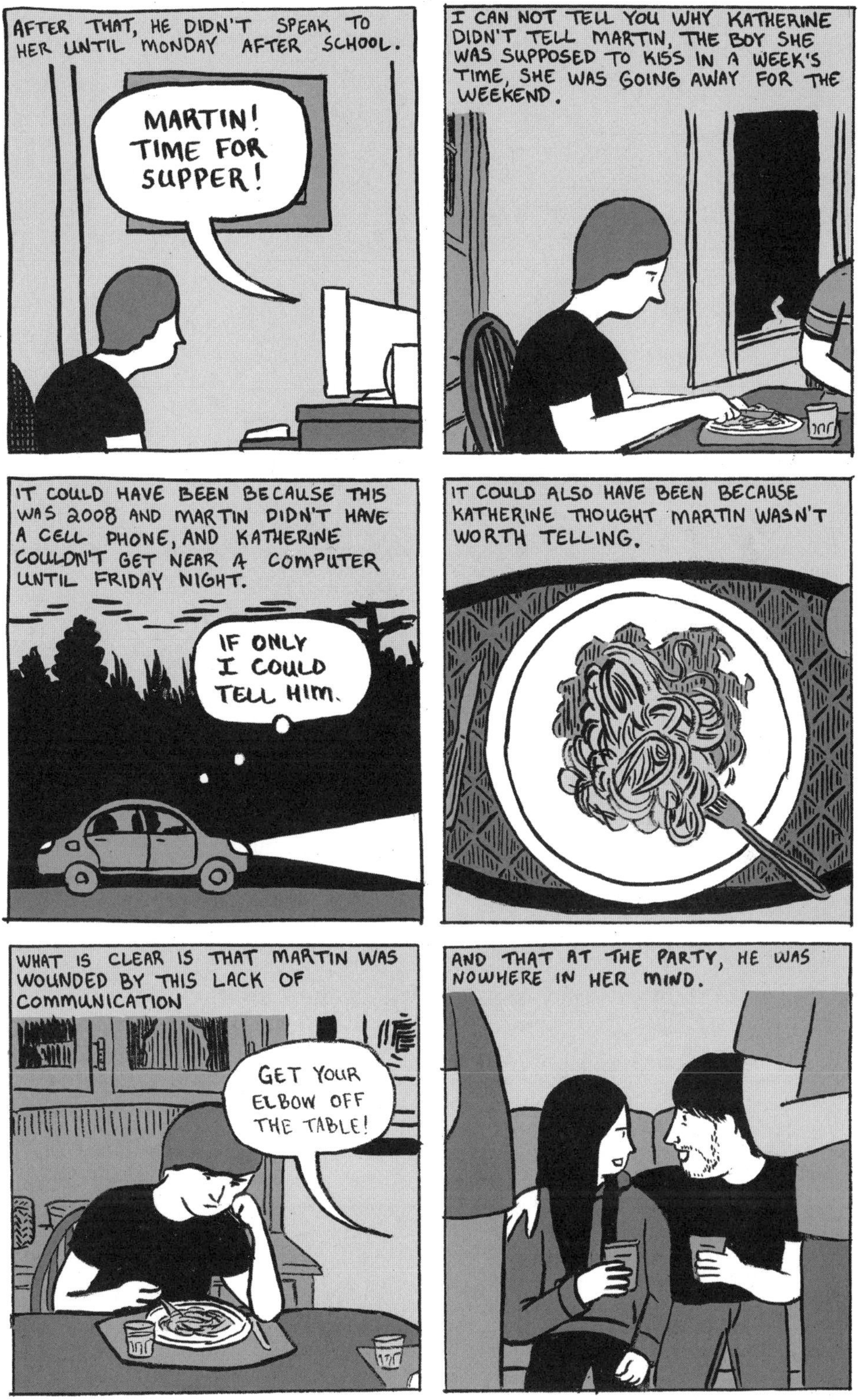
AFTER THAT, HE DIDN'T SPEAK TO HER UNTIL MONDAY AFTER SCHOOL.
MARTIN! TIME FOR SUPPER!
I CAN NOT TELL YOU WHY KATHERINE DIDN'T TELL MARTIN, THE BOY SHE WAS SUPPOSED TO KISS IN A WEEK'S TIME, SHE WAS GOING AWAY FOR THE WEEKEND.
IT COULD HAVE BEEN BECAUSE THIS WAS 2008 AND MARTIN DIDN'T HAVE A CELL PHONE, AND KATHERINE COULDN'T GET NEAR A COMPUTER UNTIL FRIDAY NIGHT.
IF ONLY I COULD TELL HIM.
IT COULD ALSO HAVE BEEN BECAUSE KATHERINE THOUGHT MARTIN WASN'T WORTH TELLING.
WHAT IS CLEAR IS THAT MARTIN WAS WOUNDED BY THIS LACK OF COMMUNICATION
GET YOUR ELBOW OFF THE TABLE!
AND THAT AT THE PARTY, HE WAS NOWHERE IN HER MIND.

OBVIOUSLY, I DON'T HAVE A FIRST-HAND ACCOUNT OF WHAT HAPPENED AT THAT PARTY,

BUT THE SPECIFIC DETAILS AREN'T IMPORTANT.

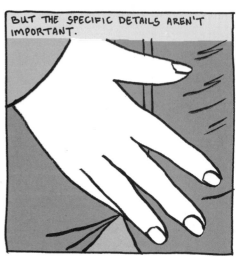

ALL WE NEED TO CONCERN OURSELVES WITH IS THE FACT THAT KATHERINE REGRETTED WHAT HAPPENED,

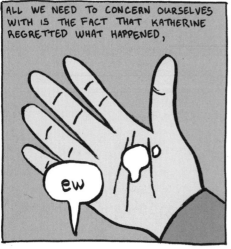

ew

AND TRIED TO FIGURE OUT WHAT TO DO ABOUT MARTIN WHEN SHE GOT BACK TO FREDERICTON.

SHE SPENT NIGHTS FIGHTING HER GUILT,

AND EVENTUALLY DECIDED TO COME CLEAN.

HEY

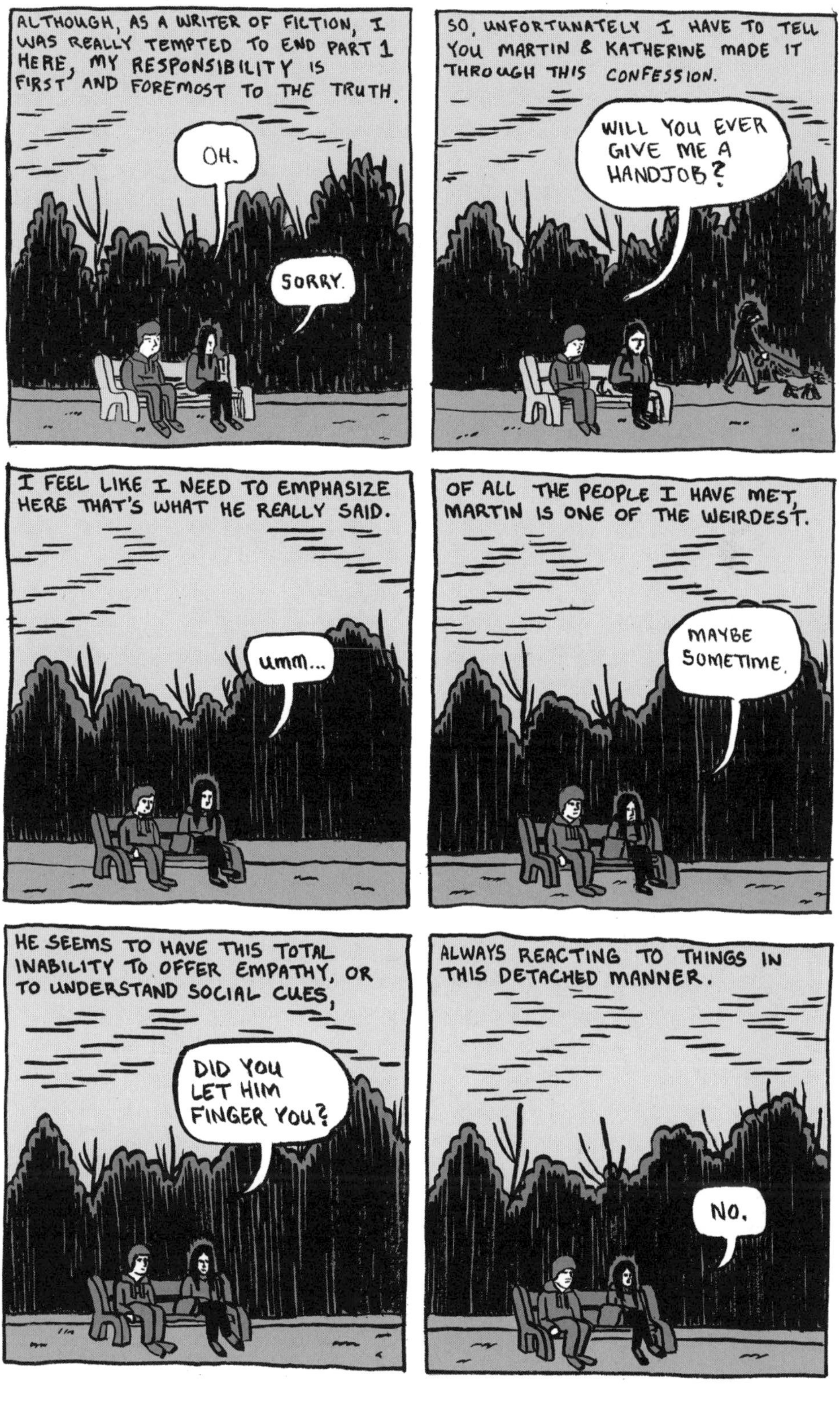
ALTHOUGH, AS A WRITER OF FICTION, I WAS REALLY TEMPTED TO END PART 1 HERE, MY RESPONSIBILITY IS FIRST AND FOREMOST TO THE TRUTH.
OH.
SORRY.
SO, UNFORTUNATELY I HAVE TO TELL YOU MARTIN & KATHERINE MADE IT THROUGH THIS CONFESSION.
WILL YOU EVER GIVE ME A HANDJOB?
I FEEL LIKE I NEED TO EMPHASIZE HERE THAT'S WHAT HE REALLY SAID.
umm...
OF ALL THE PEOPLE I HAVE MET, MARTIN IS ONE OF THE WEIRDEST.
MAYBE SOMETIME.
HE SEEMS TO HAVE THIS TOTAL INABILITY TO OFFER EMPATHY, OR TO UNDERSTAND SOCIAL CUES,
DID YOU LET HIM FINGER YOU?
ALWAYS REACTING TO THINGS IN THIS DETACHED MANNER.
NO.

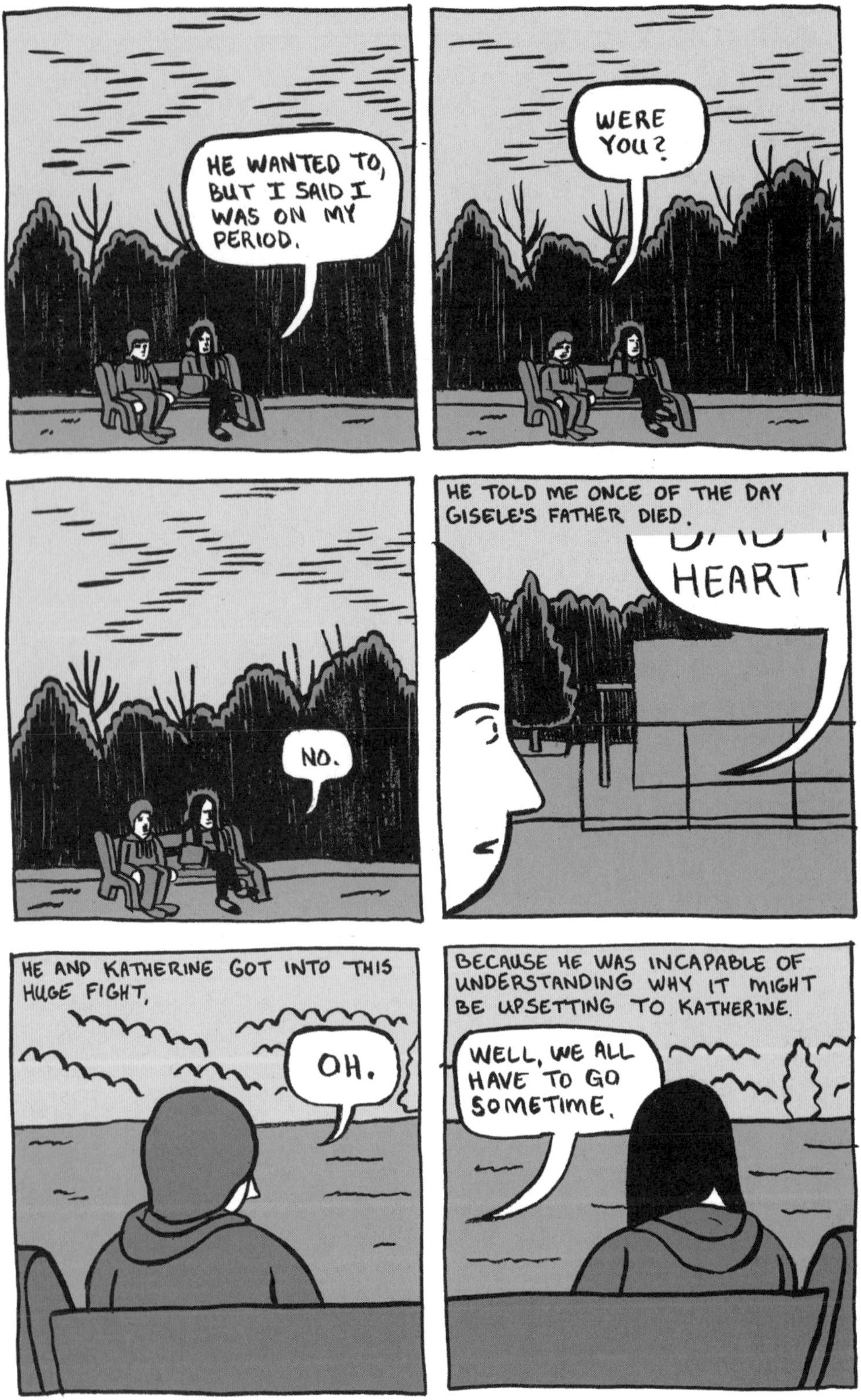
HE WANTED TO, BUT I SAID I WAS ON MY PERIOD.
WERE YOU?
NO.
HE TOLD ME ONCE OF THE DAY GISELE'S FATHER DIED.
HEART
HE AND KATHERINE GOT INTO THIS HUGE FIGHT,
OH.
BECAUSE HE WAS INCAPABLE OF UNDERSTANDING WHY IT MIGHT BE UPSETTING TO KATHERINE.
WELL, WE ALL HAVE TO GO SOMETIME.

TO THINK OF THE GRIEF THAT GISELE WOULD BE FEELING,

WAS HE FAT?

AND TO BE TOTALLY UNABLE TO HELP.

WHY DOES THAT MATTER?

BUT THAT'S BESIDE THE POINT.

EVEN THOUGH THEY STAYED TOGETHER AFTER THE HANDJOB INCIDENT,

umm

THINGS STARTED GOING DOWNHILL.

I SHOULD GO...

I THINK KATHERINE WAS HOPING MARTIN WOULD BREAK UP WITH HER, OR MAYBE GUILT HER ABOUT IT AND MAKE HER FEEL OK BREAKING UP WITH HIM.

BUT HIS REACTION JUST MADE HER LOSE RESPECT FOR HIM. WHY WOULD SHE GIVE A HANDJOB TO A GUY WHO COULDN'T EVEN MAKE A MOVE ON HER?

AND SO, AS THE DAYS WENT BY, SHE BECAME INCREASINGLY DISTANT.

∨ Online (4)
James Stewart
Grant Watson
Gisele
Alicia O'Toole
∨ Offline (32)
Katherine Paul

MARTIN FOUND HIMSELF WAITING HOURS FOR HER TO GO ONLINE,

OR WALKING AROUND THE NEIGHBOURHOOD HOPING TO BUMP INTO HER.

SOME DAYS, HE WOULD HANG OUT WITH HER FRIENDS AT LUNCH, WONDERING WHERE SHE WAS.

DON'T YOU HAVE FRIENDS?

BY THE TIME THE WINTER FORMAL CAME AROUND, THEY HADN'T SPOKEN IN OVER A WEEK.

IN FACT, THEY DIDN'T EVEN GO TOGETHER, HE JUST SHOWED UP BESIDE HER AS SHE WAS GOING IN,

HEY.

AND HE FOLLOWED HER AROUND FOR AN HOUR-AND-A-HALF, RAMBLING ABOUT HOW RADIOHEAD WAS THE NEW PINK FLOYD, AS SHE KEPT TRYING TO ESCAPE HIM.

HE HAD GONE FROM A BOYFRIEND TO A STALKER,

MORE PEST THAN MAN.

WHERE ARE YOU GOING?

IF HE WASN'T GOING TO GET HER DRIFT,

WELL — WHAT DO YOU WANT TO DO?

SHE FIGURED MAYBE SHE SHOULD JUST END IT.

CAN WE STILL BE FRIENDS?

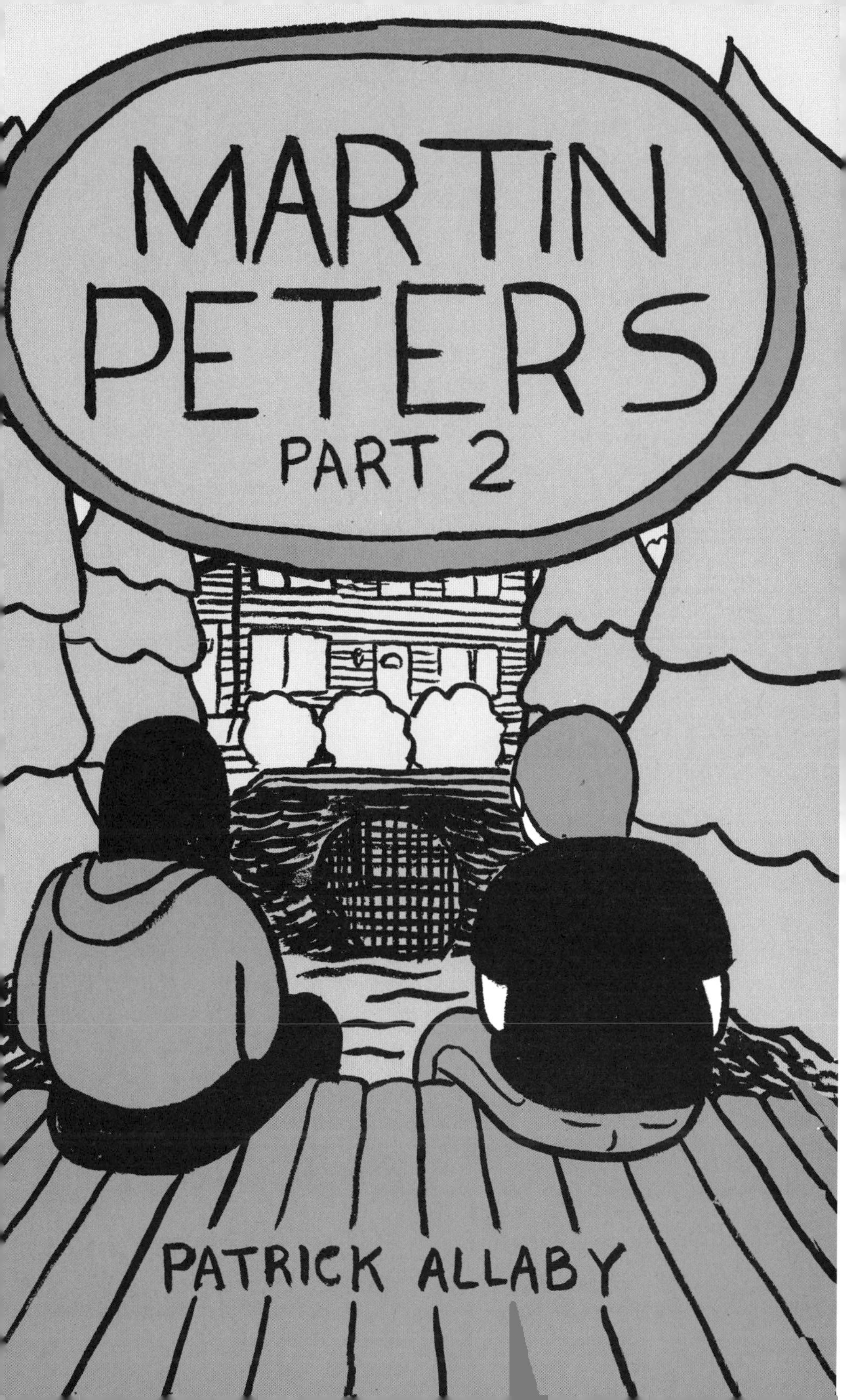
MARTIN PETERS
PART 2
PATRICK ALLABY

I FINISHED PART ONE OF MARTIN PETERS ON FEBRUARY 12, 2017,

AT WHICH POINT, I SCANNED ALL 150 DRAWINGS,

ASSEMBLED EACH OF THE 24 PAGES WITH GIMP (I'M USING THE CHESTER BROWN METHOD HERE).

AND PRINTED OUT A COPY FOR MARTIN TO SEE.

MARTIN PETERS PART 1

ON THE NEXT BLIZZARDLESS DAY, I DUG OUT MY CAR

AND DROVE TO MONCTON TO SHOW MARTIN WHAT I'D DONE.

FREDERICTON

MONCTON

SACKVILLE

SAINT JOHN

PR IS

NOV SCO

⏱ 35 min
417.5 km

MARTIN'S WIFE WAS OUT,

HEY.

BUT HE DID INTRODUCE ME TO HIS 12-MONTH-OLD DAUGHTER

HI

BEFORE WE GOT DOWN TO BUSINESS.

JUST OVER HERE.

MARTIN MADE A NUMBER OF SUGGESTIONS ABOUT HOW TO MAKE PART 1 MORE ACCURATE.

IT'S GOOD. I LIKE IT A LOT, BUT I'M WORRIED YOU'RE MAKING ME COME ACROSS KINDA BAD IN A FEW PLACES.

DESPITE THE CONCERNS I HAD ABOUT HOW THESE WILL EFFECT HOW YOU INTERPRET THIS WORK, I HAVE REVISED PART 1 AND INCLUDED MARTIN'S SUGGESTIONS.

DURING ONE OF OUR MEETINGS, MARTIN ALLUDED TO THE FACT THAT HE HAD ANOTHER GIRLFRIEND INBETWEEN THE WINTER FORMAL AND THE NEXT TIME HE SPOKE TO KATHERINE, BUT DID NOT PROVIDE ANY SPECIFICS OTHER THAN HER NAME: BECKY.

HE ALSO MENTIONED THAT FOR TWO YEARS DURING THAT PERIOD, KATHERINE HAD A PRETTY SERIOUS BOYFRIEND.

IT'S NOT CLEAR TO ME IF THAT BOYFRIEND IS THE ONE SHE GAVE A HANDJOB TO.

FOR MONTHS, KATHERINE DIDN'T TAKE THE BUS,

BUT WOULD HEAD OVER TO HER BOYFRIEND'S AFTER SCHOOL, OFTEN STAYING THE NIGHT.

HEY.

WHEN SHE FINALLY TOOK THE BUS AGAIN IN LATE MAY OF 2011, IT WAS A SIGN HER FIRST SERIOUS RELATIONSHIP WAS OVER.

MIND IF I SIT HERE?

I CAN ONLY IMAGINE WHAT IT WAS LIKE TRYING TO START A CONVERSATION STOPPED MID-SENTENCE TWO-AND-A-HALF YEARS EARLIER.

I DON'T THINK I'VE EVER GONE THAT LONG WITHOUT SPEAKING TO A CLOSE FRIEND OF MINE.

SO ...

I MEAN, WHERE DO YOU PICK UP?

ARE YOU STILL DATING THAT GUY?

HOW MANY TIMES DID YOU CHEAT ON ME?

I NEVER TOLD YOU I LOVE YOU.

CAN I HAVE THAT HAND JOB?

ARE ANY OF THOSE OLD CONVERSATION TOPICS STILL RELEVANT?

DO YOU STILL LIKE PINK FLOYD?

ALTHOUGH THEY HAD BOTH MOVED ON IN THEIR MUSICAL TASTES,

NOT REALLY.

IT DIDN'T TAKE THEM LONG TO FIND COMMON GROUND.

SO DO YOU SMOKE WEED?

KATHERINE AND HER OTHER BOYFRIEND
WERE WELL-KNOWN STONERS AROUND
FREDERICTON HIGH SCHOOL —

UP TO THE POINT THAT AT LEAST
ONE OF THEM WAS ALWAYS WEARING
ONE OF THOSE PONCHO HOODIES —

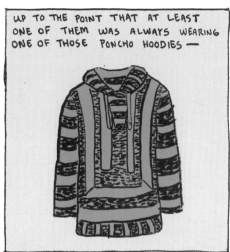

AND MARTIN'S BRAGGING ABOUT HIS
WEED-SMOKING HABITS WAS LESS
FACT THAN IT WAS AN ELABORATE
FICTION CONCOCTED TO IMPRESS HER.

HAVE YOU
EVER DONE
A YETI?

IT WASN'T JUST THAT HE'D
ONLY HAD A HANDFUL OF OPPORTUNI-
TIES UP UNTIL THAT POINT TO GET
HIGH,

ARE YOU GUYS
SMOKING WEED?

MAN,
SEEN
AFGH
HAO

BUT ALSO, OUT OF FEAR, HE'D
TURNED DOWN EVERY OPPORTUNITY
TO SMOKE UP THAT HAD PRESENTED
ITSELF TO HIM THUS FAR.

YOU WANT
A HIT?

HOWEVER, HE HAD GLEANED ENOUGH
FROM HIS FRIENDS TO FAKE IT IN
FRONT OF KATHERINE.

GIVE ME THE
GANJA IF THE
LIL' PUSS' IS
TOO CHICKEN
TO TOKE UP.

NOT ONLY DID MARTIN LARGELY REFRAIN FROM SMOKING WEED IN HIGH SCHOOL, HE HAD ALSO DRANK ONLY ONCE BY THE END OF GRADE 12.

IT WAS DURING THE GRADE 11 INCARNATION OF HIS FRIEND WILL'S ANNUAL CHRISTMAS PARTY. HE HAD A SINGLE RUM AND DIET COKE AND WAS SO SCARED HE STAYED UP ALL NIGHT TESTING HIS BLOOD SUGAR HOURLY.

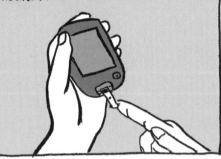

MARTIN'S TREPIDATIONS ABOUT SMOKING WEED AND DRINKING CAME BOTH FROM FEAR; HE DIDN'T SMOKE BECAUSE HE WAS AFRAID OF BREAKING THE LAW, WHILE HE DIDN'T DRINK BECAUSE HE WAS SCARED OF DYING.

AT HIS DOCTOR'S APPOINTMENT RIGHT BEFORE THE GRADE ELEVEN CHRISTMAS PARTY, HE LEARNT FROM HIS ENDOCRINOLOGIST WHAT ALCOHOL CAN DO TO A DIABETIC.

SO, MARTIN, AT THIS POINT IN YOUR LIFE, YOU MAY BE EXPOSED TO ALCOHOL AND THERE'S SOME THINGS YOU SHOULD KNOW...

YOU SEE, A DIABETIC'S KIDNEYS CAN'T PROCESS ALCOHOL AND SUGAR AT THE SAME TIME

AND IF YOU DRINK TOO MUCH, YOUR KIDNEYS WILL STOP RELEASING SUGAR AND YOUR BLOOD SUGAR LEVELS CAN COME CRASHING DOWN TO POTENTIALLY DISASTEROUS RESULTS, INCLUDING DEATH.

ONE OF THE THINGS THAT STOOD OUT MOST TO MARTIN ABOUT KATHERINE THE FIRST TIME THEY DATED IS THAT SHE'D NEVER SEEN STAR WARS.

ARE YOU SERIOUS?

MARTIN HAD IN HIS POSSESSION BACK THEN TWO COPIES OF A V.H.S. BOX SET OF THE ORIGINAL TRILOGY,

ONE OF WHICH HE GAVE TO KATHERINE BACK IN GRADE 10.

IS THIS REALLY NECESSARY?

DURING A LULL IN THEIR CONVERSATION, IN WHICH MARTIN HAD EXHAUSTED HIS KNOWLEDGE OF MARIJUANA,

WHAT SHOULD I SAY NOW?

EXIT

HE WAS SCOURING HIS BRAIN FOR SOMETHING, SOME CONVERSATION TOPIC THAT THEY COULD PICK UP,

FLOYD BAT
MOVI
EED KATHERINE
RUGS LSD SH SE
STAR PROM
WARS

WHEN THERE, DEEP IN THE RECESSES OF HIS MIND, MARTIN FOUND STAR WARS.

HEY, DID YOU EVER WATCH THAT STAR WARS BOX SET I LENT YOU?

EXIT

TO MARTIN'S AMAZEMENT, IN THE TWO-AND-A-HALF YEARS SINCE HE HAD GIVEN HER THAT BOX SET, KATHERINE HAD NOT BOTHERED TO WATCH THE ORIGINAL TRILOGY A SINGLE TIME!

YOU KNOW THEY'RE LIKE THE GREATEST MOVIES OF ALL TIME!?

SO, HE INVITED HER OVER TO WATCH THEM,

BUT FOUND SHE WAS SOON BORED.

DID YOU SEE THAT!?

TO BREAK UP THE TEDIUM, THEY WOULD GO FOR WALKS IN BETWEEN MOVIES,

COME ON!

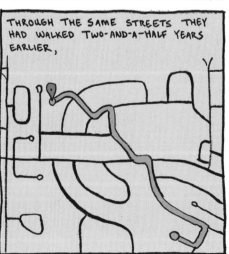

THROUGH THE SAME STREETS THEY HAD WALKED TWO-AND-A-HALF YEARS EARLIER,

STOPPING HERE AND THERE TO GET HIGH.

MARTIN DIDN'T OWN ANY WEED PARAPHERNALIA OF HIS OWN AND WAS FORCED TO RELY ON WHAT KATHERINE HAD IN HER BAG.

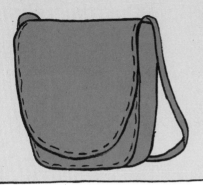

WITH HER YEARS OF EXPERIENCE, KATHERINE HAD ACCUMULATED QUITE AN INFRASTRUCTURE FOR SMOKING WEED.

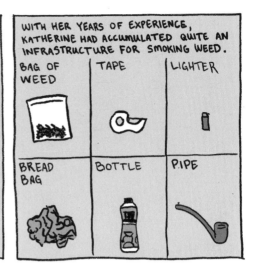

BAG OF WEED	TAPE	LIGHTER
BREAD BAG	BOTTLE	PIPE

SHE WAS PARTICULARLY ADEPT AT MAKING LUNGS AND THROUGHOUT THE EXAM PERIOD, VARIOUS DEVICES ACCUMULATED AROUND THE BRIDGE THEY SMOKED ON. THERE WAS THE TWO-LITRE POP BOTTLE,

THE MINUTE MADE ORANGE JUICE BOTTLE

AND THE POP CAN PIPE.

HOWEVER, HER FAVOURITE THING TO SMOKE OUT OF WAS A PURPLE PIPE SHE KEPT IN HER BAG.

(OBJECTS NOT DRAWN TO SCALE)

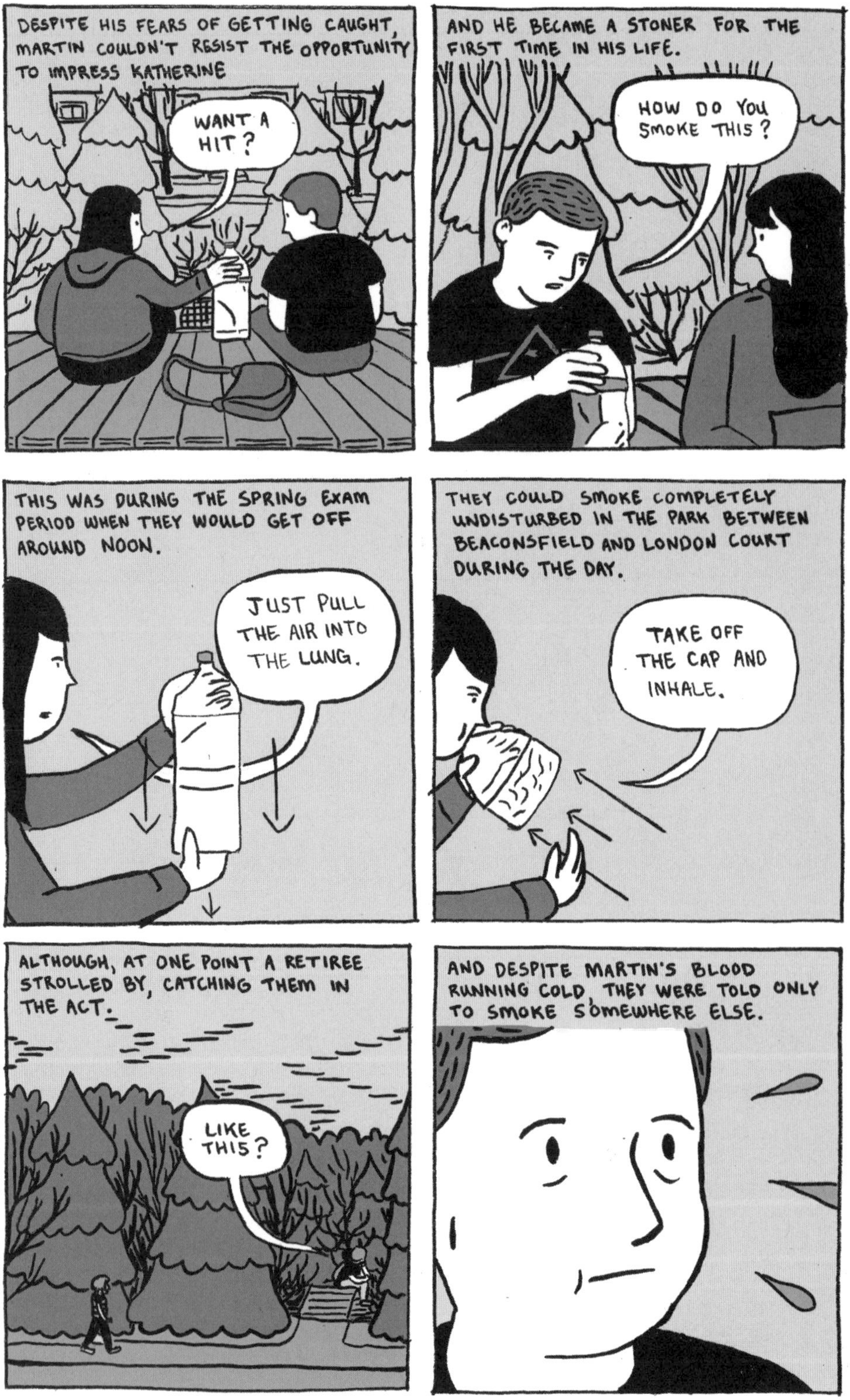
DESPITE HIS FEARS OF GETTING CAUGHT, MARTIN COULDN'T RESIST THE OPPORTUNITY TO IMPRESS KATHERINE
WANT A HIT?
AND HE BECAME A STONER FOR THE FIRST TIME IN HIS LIFE.
HOW DO YOU SMOKE THIS?
THIS WAS DURING THE SPRING EXAM PERIOD WHEN THEY WOULD GET OFF AROUND NOON.
JUST PULL THE AIR INTO THE LUNG.
THEY COULD SMOKE COMPLETELY UNDISTURBED IN THE PARK BETWEEN BEACONSFIELD AND LONDON COURT DURING THE DAY.
TAKE OFF THE CAP AND INHALE.
ALTHOUGH, AT ONE POINT A RETIREE STROLLED BY, CATCHING THEM IN THE ACT.
LIKE THIS?
AND DESPITE MARTIN'S BLOOD RUNNING COLD, THEY WERE TOLD ONLY TO SMOKE SOMEWHERE ELSE.

THE PURPLE PIPE MET ITS MAKER ON MARTIN AND KATHERINE'S FIRST REAL DATE,

I WOULD NEVER WANT TO LIVE IN THOSE APARTMENTS.

FOR WHICH THEY WENT TO A SHOW AT THE CHARLOTTE STREET ARTS CENTRE.

I FEEL LIKE WE'RE GOING TO BE VERY EARLY.

WH TI IS

ON THE WALK DOWN THEY DECIDED TO STOP AND SMOKE A BOWL IN A CULVERT OFF THE BEAVERBROOK ST. WALKING TRAIL.

AT ONE POINT, AS FATE WOULD HAVE IT, IT OCCURRED TO MARTIN HOW EASILY THE PIPE COULD BREAK ON THE CONCRETE SURFACE THEY STOOD ON.

IT WOULD SUCK IF YOU DROPPED THIS PIPE.

AS HE PASSED IT BACK TO KATHERINE FOR SAFEKEEPING,

MAYBE YOU SHOULD HOLD ONTO IT.

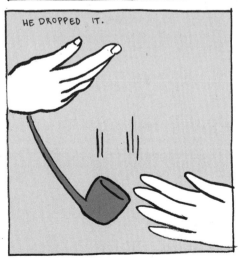

HE DROPPED IT.

IT WAS NOT A GOOD START FOR THEM.

DON'T FREAK OUT! I'LL GET YOU A NEW ONE!!

FORTUNATELY, KATHERINE'S FRIEND GISELE WAS THERE TO EASE THE TENSION.

GISELE!

IN THE PARKING LOT, GISELE, WHO HAD RECENTLY BROKEN UP WITH HER BOYFRIEND OF OVER A YEAR, ASKED MARTIN IF HE COULD SET HER UP WITH A FRIEND OF HIS

DO YOU THINK HE'D WANT TO FUCK ME?

AND WENT ON TO DESCRIBE HOW UNSATISFYING HER SEX LIFE HAD BEEN.

FROM NOW ON, I'm IMPOSING A NO SMALL DICKS RULE! I MEAN I COULD BARELY TELL WHEN TOM WAS INSIDE ME!!!

SHE SPOKE OF HER EX — A FRIEND OF MARTIN'S — AS A SLOPPY AND CARELESS LOVER.

EXCEPT THAT TIME HE PUT IT IN THE WRONG HOLE! IT HURT SO MUCH I WENT BLACK!!

MARTIN HAD NEVER HEARD A WOMAN BE SO OVERTLY SEXUAL.

LIKE IS IT TOO MUCH TO ASK FOR A GOOD FUCK!?

AS WITH ANY HIGH SCHOOL LOVE STORY, PROM PLAYS AN IMPORTANT ROLE IN MARTIN'S.

ALTHOUGH THEY DIDN'T GO TO PROM TOGETHER (MARTIN HAVING FOUND A DATE IN MID-MARCH), MARTIN AND KATHERINE ENDED UP HANGING OUT TOGETHER AFTERWARDS.

YOU SEE, MARTIN'S MOM THOUGHT IT WOULD BE TOO DANGEROUS FOR HIM TO BE AROUND SO MUCH DRINKING AT THE AFTER-PARTY

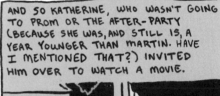

I DON'T WANT TO GET SOME CALL AT THREE IN THE MORNING TELLING ME YOU'RE IN THE HOSPITAL!!!

AND SO KATHERINE, WHO WASN'T GOING TO PROM OR THE AFTER-PARTY (BECAUSE SHE WAS, AND STILL IS, A YEAR YOUNGER THAN MARTIN. HAVE I MENTIONED THAT?) INVITED HIM OVER TO WATCH A MOVIE.

THIS WAS THE FIRST TIME MARTIN HAD EVER BEEN TO KATHERINE'S HOUSE,

WHICH, HE FOUND REMARKABLY SIMILAR TO HIS OWN.

HI

HEY.

ALL THAT MARTIN REMEMBERS OF THE MOVIE IS IT STARRED JOHNNY DEPP AND LOOKED ODDLY DATED.

AS FAR AS HE WAS CONCERNED, THE FILM WAS COMPLETE TRASH, BUT KATHERINE SEEMED ODDLY INTERESTED IN IT.

HE'S JUST SOO—

GOOD.

HOWEVER, BEFORE LONG, THEIR CONVERSATION OVERTOOK THE MOVIE

NOW THAT'S A QUESTIONABLE STATEMENT!

BUT WHAT ABOUT HIS RUGGED BEAUTY?

AND THEY DREW CLOSER AND CLOSER TO EACH OTHER

YOU KNOW, PEOPLE SAY I LOOK LIKE JOHNNY DEPP.

NO THEY DON'T!! YOU LOOK LIKE MICHAEL CERA.

BEFORE FINALLY, AFTER TWO-AND-A-HALF YEARS,

OH.

MICHAEL CERA'S GOOD THOUGH

SHARING THEIR FIRST KISS.

IT FELT TO MARTIN LIKE HE HAD WAITED FOR THIS HIS ENTIRE LIFE.

THAT IT WAS SOMETHING HE WAS BORN FOR,

AND, AS HE KISSED KATHERINE, HE COULDN'T HELP BUT THINK OF HIS FIFTEEN-YEAR-OLD SELF MASTURBATING TO THIS VERY MOMENT BACK ALONG HIS SPACE-TIME CONTINUUM.

UP UNTIL THIS POINT, THINGS LIKE THE TASTE OF HER MOUTH,

OR THE SIZE OF HER BREASTS,

HAD BEEN THE STUFF OF DREAMS.

HOWEVER, LIKE THE ARRIVAL OF A LONG-RUMOURED SEQUEL TO A CLASSIC ACTION MOVIE,

MARTIN COULDN'T HELP BUT BE DISAPPOINTED BY THE PHYSICAL MANIFESTATION OF KATHERINE'S BODY

AND BY THE FACT SHE BARELY JERKED HIM OFF.

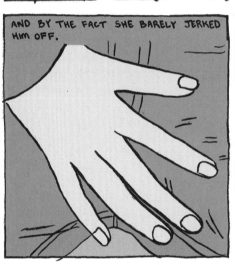

FORTUNATELY THOUGH, THIS WAS ONLY THE BEGINNING OF THEIR SUMMER ROMANCE

AND THEY HAD PLENTY MORE CHANCES TO GO TO WHERE THE WATER AND THE EARTH CARESS.

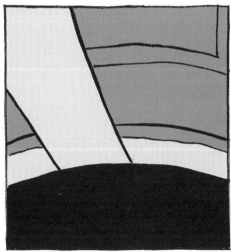

A CORE DIFFERENCE BETWEEN THIS SUMMER ROMANCE AND THE FALL OF 2008 WAS THAT MARTIN AND KATHERINE WERE NO LONGER CONFINED TO SKYLINE ACRES.

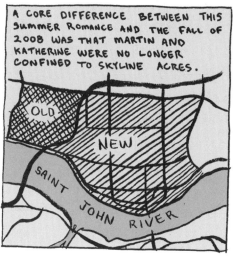

I MEAN THE DIFFERENCE WAS PRIMARILY PSYCHOLOGICAL. THERE WERE NO PHYSICAL BARRIERS KEEPING THEM IN SKYLINE BACK THEN.

DO YOU WANT TO KEEP GOING?

IT'S NOT LIKE THERE WERE FENCES, OR SOMETHING, HOLDING THEM IN.

I WISH WE COULD.

FINALLY, AFTER YEARS OF GOOD BEHAVIOUR, MARTIN'S PARENTS HAD STARTED TO TRUST HIM, AND WOULD NO LONGER GO LOOKING FOR HIM AFTER AN HOUR.

SURE.

OFTEN, THEY WOULD WALK DOWN TO THE RIVER TOWARDS MORELL PARK,

FUCKIN' MOSQUITOS!

SMACK!

WHY WE C THIS

WHERE THEY COULD USUALLY FIND FRIENDS OF MARTIN'S SMOKING UP.

TO GET AROUND THE OBVIOUS CRIMINALITY OF SMOKING WEED IN PUBLIC,

HEY

SUP, MY DUDES?

MARTIN'S FRIEND WILL HAD INVESTED IN A HOOKAH,

AND MIXED IN WEED WITH THE STRONGER SMELLING SHISHA.

MAN...

THAT WAY, ANYTIME A POLICE OFFICER DECIDED TO CHECK OUT THE SUSPICIOUS-LOOKING VEHICLE PARKED BY THE RIVER,

FULL OF TEENS ON SUMMER BREAK,

UH-OH.

HE COULD FIND NOTHING ILLEGAL.

NOT MUCH, BRA!

SNIFF SNIFF

LOOK, I WAS HOPING TO AVOID THIS, BUT WORKING WITH MARTIN HAS BECOME INCREDIBLY DIFFICULT SINCE I FINISHED PART ONE.

IT'S LIKE HE'S BEEN STANDING OVER MY SHOULDER FOR THE PAST TWO MONTHS.

I'VE BEEN DRAWING THIS IN THE EVENINGS AFTER WORK (GALLERY INTERN, OWENS ART GALLERY), COMPLETING ABOUT TWO PAGES PER WEEK.

EVERY WEEK SINCE I SHOWED HIM PART ONE, MARTIN'S BEEN GETTING ME TO SCAN WHAT I'VE DONE AND SEND IT TO HIM

AND HE'D MESSAGE ME BACK WITH ALL THESE SUGGESTIONS TO "MAKE IT MORE ACCURATE"

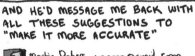

AND I WOULD MAKE THE APPROPRIATE CHANGES.

AT FIRST, THIS FELT LIKE A MINOR INCONVENIENCE. I HAD DONE MY BEST TO BE FAITHFUL TO WHAT MARTIN HAD TOLD ME AND FIGURED I MIS-REMEMBERED A FEW THINGS HERE AND THERE.

WAS IT:

SO, I HAD TO GET HER TO SHOW ME HOW TO SMOKE A LUNG!

OR:

SO, I WOULD SIT THERE AS SHE'D SMOKE UP

?

BUT, WITH RECENT PAGES DEPICTING HIS MARIJUANA USE, IT'S BECOME CLEAR THAT HE WOULD RATHER SEE A FICTIONAL VERSION OF HIMSELF

THAN THE FLAWED YOUNG DIABETIC WHOSE STORY I WAS INTERESTED IN TELLING IN THE FIRST PLACE.

AND THE WHOLE TIME I JUST KEPT THINKING, "MAN, WHAT WOULD MY ENDOCRINOLOGIST SAY IF SHE KNEW I HAD BECOME A POT-HEAD?"!

AND BECAUSE I KNOW HE WOULD TAKE SERIOUS ISSUE WITH HOW I AM GOING TO PORTRAY HIM OVER THE NEXT FEW PAGES, I HAVE DECIDED TO CUT OFF CONTACT WITH HIM.

I HAVE ALSO GONE BACK IN AND TAKEN OUT HIS EARLIER EDITS. IN ORDER TO TELL THIS STORY FULLY, TRUTHFULLY, AND WITHOUT COMPROMISE.

SUFFICE IT TO SAY, THE PRODUCT YOU HOLD IN YOUR HANDS IS THE REAL STORY OF MARTIN PETERS, AS IT WAS ORIGINALLY TOLD TO ME.

SO, BACK TO OUR MAIN STORY, I WANTED TO TELL YOU A LITTLE BIT ABOUT KATHERINE'S OLDER BROTHER, CHRIS.

HI. I'M CHRIS.

TWO YEARS OLDER THAN KATHERINE AND ONE YEAR OLDER THAN MARTIN, CHRIS HAD GRADUATED FROM HIGH SCHOOL THE YEAR BEFORE AND STILL LIVED AT HOME.

HEY.

AS A RESULT, KATHERINE WOULD OFTEN TRY — WITH A REASONABLY HIGH SUCCESS RATE — TO PURSUADE HIM TO DRIVE HER AND HER FRIENDS AROUND TOWN

CAN YOU TAKE US TO LISA'S?

AND, EVEN WHEN HE WAS UNCOMFORTABLE WITH WHAT SHE WAS DOING, HE WOULD BE MORE THAN HAPPY TO OBLIGE.

CAN YOU STOP SMOKING BACK THERE!

IN LATE JULY, KATHERINE MANAGED TO GET CHRIS TO DRIVE HER AND MARTIN TO A PARTY OUT IN HANWELL,

WHICH WAS SHAPING UP TO BE THE PARTY OF THE SUMMER.

THROUGHOUT HIGH SCHOOL, MARTIN HAD SAT PATIENTLY IN HOMEROOM ON MONDAY MORNINGS AS THE PREVIOUS WEEKEND'S PARTIES WERE DISCUSSED IN DETAIL.

THEY WERE MAKING OUT LIKE THE ENTIRE NIGHT!

THEN, AT BREAK, HE'D GET TO HEAR WHICH OF HIS FRIENDS HAD DONE WHAT ON THE WILD NIGHT.

...AND BALCOM WAS BEGGIN' HIM TO PUNCH HIM!

BA A F

SOMETIMES, DURING A SLOW NEWS WEEK, THE CONVERSATIONS WOULD CONTINUE INTO TUESDAY OR, GOD FORGIVE, WEDNESDAY.

SO, PETER SAYS THAT SHE ALREADY HAS A BOYFRIEND, BUT MATT DOESN'T KNOW!

OCCASIONALLY, SOMEONE WOULD CASUALLY LAMENT THE FACT THAT MARTIN HAD NOT WITNESSED THESE EPIC EVENTS,

MAN, YOU SHOULDA BEEN THERE!

IT WAS DOPE

AND HE'D ALWAYS BE SURE TO CALL THEM OUT ON THEIR INSINCERITY.

WELL, ONE OF YOU CUNTS SHOULD HAVE INVITED ME!

WELL, AT LEAST IN HIS HEAD.

YEAH

!#@^

ANYWAYS, THIS WAS ESSENTIALLY MARTIN'S FIRST HIGH SCHOOL PARTY

AND HE WAS OVERWHELMED BY WHAT HE SAW BEFORE HIM.

GISELE!

MARTIN LET HIMSELF INDULGE IN ALL THE WEED,

ALCOHOL,

AND DANCING HE PHYSICALLY COULD.

BUT MOSTLY, HE FOCUSED ON KATHERINE.

THE PAIR STARTED TO GET CARRIED AWAY IN THE MOMENT

AND PROCEEDED TO THE UNFINISHED BASEMENT, WHERE THEY COULD BE ALONE.

COME ON!

IT WAS IN THAT BASEMENT THAT TWO THINGS HAPPENED:

MARTIN LOST HIS VIRGINITY,

AND HIS BLOOD SUGAR CAME CRASHING DOWN.

SHUFFLE

HAVE YOU EVER WOKEN UP IN THE HOSPITAL?

BREAKFAST IS HERE...

NOT LIKE AFTER STAYING OVER NIGHT, BUT, LIKE ONE MOMENT YOU'RE DOING SOMETHING

YOU NEED TO GET HARD.

AND THE NEXT THING YOU KNOW,

IT'LL JUST BE RIGHT HERE.

YOU'RE IN A HOSPITAL BED

YOUR INSULIN AND GLUCOMETER ARE OVER HERE.

YOUR PARENTS DROPPED THEM OFF.

AND 12 HOURS HAVE GONE BY. HAS THAT EVER HAPPENED TO YOU?

THANK YOU.

IT HAPPENED TO ME IN MY FIRST YEAR OF UNIVERSITY.

I HAD ALCOHOL POISONING FROM A PERFORMANCE ART PIECE.

I WAS TRYING TO MAKE SOME KIND OF COMMENTARY ON TOXIC MASCULINITY BY WRITING "I'M NOT A PUSSY" OVER AND OVER AGAIN, WHILE SIMULTANEOUSLY GETTING SO DRUNK I THREW UP ON THE DRAWING, PROVING THAT I WAS, IN FACT, A PUSSY.

THE THING IS, I WAS SLOW TO PUKE,

SO MY FRIENDS STARTED FORCING ALCOHOL DOWN MY THROAT

AND THE NEXT THING I KNEW, I WAS IN A HOSPITAL BED BEING ASKED TO LEAVE BECAUSE THEY HAD RUN OUT OF SPACE.

IT'S TIME FOR YOU TO GO.

MARTIN'S TRIP, HOWEVER, WASN'T SO BRIEF.

HE WAS VISITED FIRST BY HIS PARENTS, WHO WERE BOTH UPSET

I CALLED AND I CALLED UNTIL, EVENTUALLY, THIS MAN ANSWERS AND TELLS ME THAT MY SON IS UNRESPONSIVE AND IN AN AMBULANCE! HOW DO YOU THINK THAT FEELS!?

SNIFF SN

AND ENRAGED BY HIS RECKLESSNESS.

WHILE YOU'RE LIVING IN MY HOUSE, UNDER MY ROOF, YOU'RE GOING TO BE LIVING BY MY RULES, WHICH MEANS YOU WON'T LET A SINGLE DROP OF ALCOHOL TOUCH THOSE LIPS UNTIL I SAY SO -- OR YOU'RE OUT!!!

NEXT, HIS ENDOCRINOLOGIST, WHO WAS MUCH MORE ACCUSTOMED TO SEEING YOUNG DIABETICS GET THEMSELVES IN TROUBLE, SHOWED UP AND GAVE IT TO HIM STRAIGHT.

I GET IT. YOU'RE YOUNG, YOU WANT TO PARTY. IT'S BOUND TO HAPPEN. BUT YOU HAVE TO BE RESPONSIBLE. THERE ARE THINGS YOU COULD HAVE DONE TO AVOID THIS HAPPENING. DON'T DRINK WITHOUT EATING. CARRY GLUCOSE TABLETS. WEAR A MEDIC ALERT BRACELET.

SHE ALSO LET SLIP A FEW DETAILS OF WHAT HAD HAPPENED AT THE PARTY.

LUCKILY, YOUR (um) FRIEND GISELE KNEW YOU WERE DIABETIC, BECAUSE NO ONE ELSE AT THAT PARTY SEEMED TO. IF IT WASN'T FOR HER YOU COULD BE IN A LOT WORSE SHAPE RIGHT NOW.

AND, ALTHOUGH HE WAITED FOR HER UNTIL HE WAS DISCHARGED AT 5, KATHERINE FAILED TO CHECK IN ON HIM.

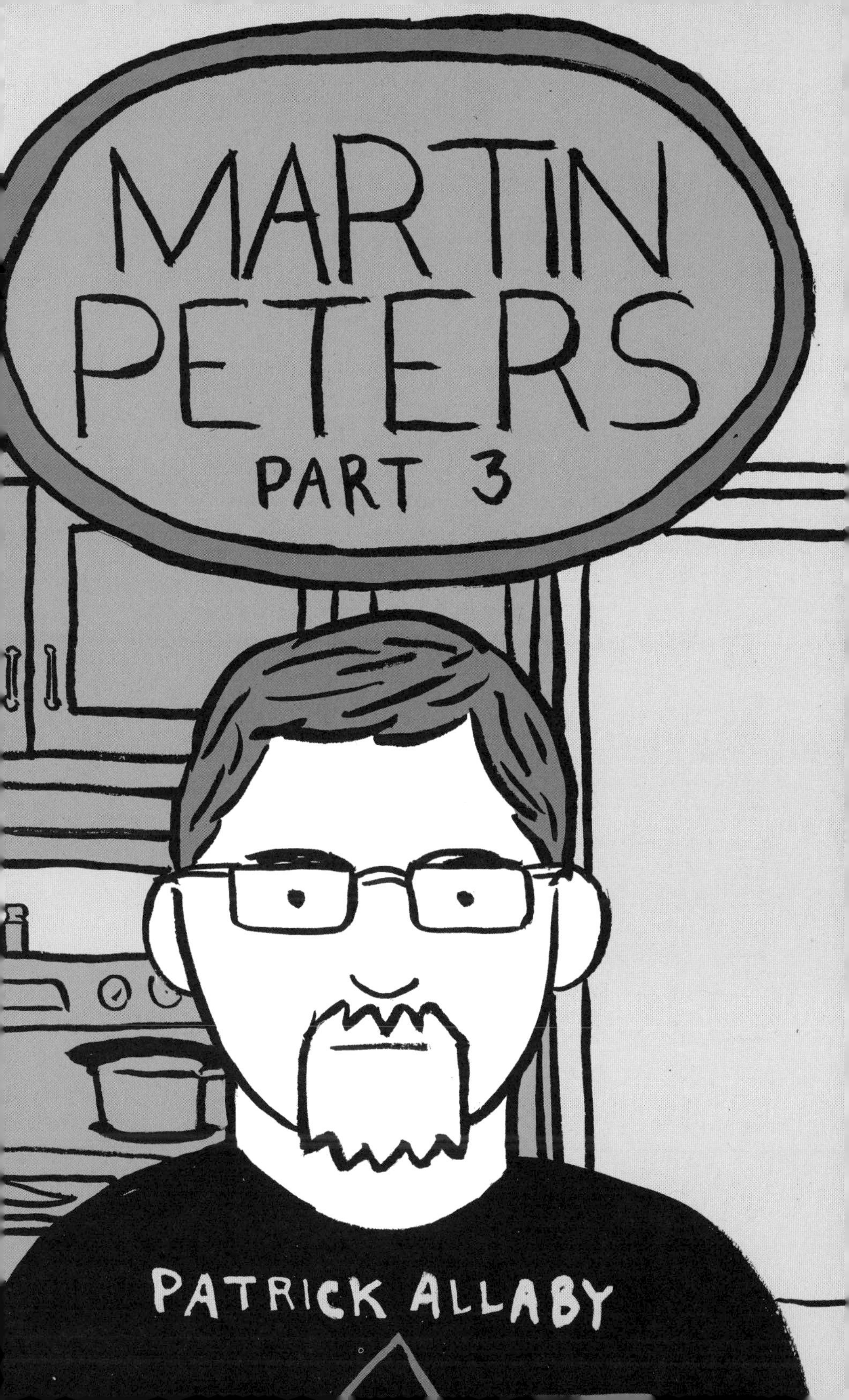
MARTIN PETERS
PART 3
PATRICK ALLABY

SO, WHILE I WAS WORKING ON PART 2 OF MARTIN PETERS, I WAS INVITED TO TABLE AT A ZINE FAIR IN FREDERICTON.

SINCE I HAD BEEN WORKING ON THIS BOOK FOR SO LONG, I DIDN'T HAVE ANYTHING NEW TO SELL.

SEPT. 2016 TO APRIL 2017 300 (ISH) DRAWINGS

I HAD ALSO SOLD OUT OF MY PREVIOUS TWO BOOKS.

SO, BECAUSE I NEEDED SOMETHING TO SELL, I DECIDED TO MAKE COPIES OF MARTIN PETERS PART 1, WHICH I'D ORIGINALLY MADE JUST FOR ITS SUBJECT.

I HAVE TO SAY, HAVING SPENT FIVE MONTHS ON PART 1, IT WAS DEEPLY SATISFYING (AND A HUGE RELIEF!) TO SEE HOW GOOD IT LOOKED.

UNFORTUNATELY, I ONLY SOLD 3 COPIES.

IT'S FIVE— BUT THAT'S NEGOTIABLE...

BUT THEN THE NEXT WEEKEND, I WAS AT A ZINE FAIR IN SAINT JOHN (FOR QUALITY BLOCK PARTY)

AND THIS REPORTER WHO RUNS AN ONLINE ARTS N' CULTURE MAGAZINE AND WHO HAD SEEN ME IN FREDERICTON BOUGHT A COPY.

I'M FROM GRID CITY

HE LIKED IT SO MUCH HE DID A PROFILE OF ME.

A Teenager In Skyline Acres

category: arts © May 9, 2017

New Brunswick comic artist Patrick Allaby +

Matt Carter

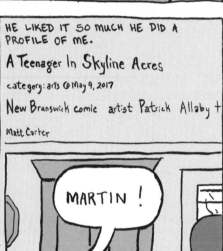

MARTIN!

BY THE TIME I RELEASED PART 2 A FEW MONTHS LATER, MARTIN PETERS HAD EVEN DEVELOPED A (VERY) SMALL FOLLOWING.

MARTIN PETERS PART 2

PATRICK ALLABY

SINCE THEN, PEOPLE HAVE BEEN COMING UP TO ME ALL OVER THE PLACE AND ASKING ABOUT MARTIN AND KATHERINE.

SO, DID THEY, LIKE, BREAK UP?

I EVEN HAD AN ART SHOW AT STRUTS GALLERY IN SACKVILLE WHERE THE ORIGINAL DRAWINGS FOR BOTH PARTS 1+2 WERE ON DISPLAY.

I FEEL LIKE I'LL REGRET SAYING THIS, BUT I WAS PRETTY PROUD OF HOW PART 2 ENDED.

AND, ALTHOUGH HE WAITED FOR HER UNTIL HE WAS DISCHARGED AT 5, KATHERINE FAILED TO CHECK IN ON HIM.

I KINDA THOUGHT I NAILED THE SEMI-AMBIGUOUS ENDING, WHERE THE STORY WAS OVER, BUT THINGS WERE STILL UP IN THE AIR.

SATISFYING, BUT NOT OVERLY.

THE PROBLEM WAS THAT PEOPLE KEPT COMING UP TO ME AND ASKING WHAT HAPPENED AFTER MARTIN GOT OUT OF THE HOSPITAL

SO, WHAT WAS HER REACTION TO MARTIN'S HOSPITALISATION?

AND I FELT LIKE A DICK ALWAYS DODGING THEIR QUESTIONS.

WELL, THAT'S FOR YOU TO DECIDE.

LIKE I'VE SAID, THIS IS NOT SOME LITERARY WORK IN WHICH THE CHARACTERS DON'T HAVE A LIFE PAST THE LAST PAGE. THIS IS NON-FICTION. COMICS JOURNALISM.

SO, I'VE MADE THIS PART 3 AS A SORT OF "WHERE ARE THEY NOW?" FOR THOSE OF YOU INTERESTED IN THAT SORT OF THING.

AS YOU PROBABLY GUESSED FROM THE LAST PANEL OF PART 2, MARTIN AND KATHERINE BROKE UP AFTER THE PARTY.

I REALIZE THAT THAT MAKES IT SOUND LIKE THEY HAD AN ACTUAL BREAK UP.

WHAT HAPPENED WAS THAT KATHERINE JUST HARD CORE STARTED GHOSTING MARTIN.

HE WOULD SEND HER ENDLESS MESSAGES

AND

NEVER ONCE HEARD BACK.

MARTIN WOULD ALSO GO FOR ENDLESS WALKS,

WHY DOESN'T SHE ANSWER ME?

TREKKING THROUGH WHERE THEY USED TO HANG OUT TOGETHER,

EVEN GOING BY HER HOUSE IN HOPES OF BUMPING INTO HER.

THE CLOSEST HE GOT WAS ONCE SEEING HER DRIVE PAST HIM ON FOREST HILL ROAD.

WHAT WAS PARTICULARLY CRUSHING ABOUT THIS WHOLE EXPERIENCE WAS THAT MARTIN KEPT SEEING PHOTOS OF HER ON FACEBOOK AT PARTIES WITH HIS FRIENDS,

WHO'D CONVENIENTLY FORGOT TO INVITE HIM.

AT SOME POINT DURING HIS QUEST FOR KATHERINE, MARTIN REMEMBERED TO THANK GISELE FOR SAVING HIS LIFE.

hey.

SOMEHOW, THIS LED THEM TO GOING TO A MOVIE TOGETHER

HEY

AND GETTING ALONG WONDERFULLY.

Chap

DO YOU WANT TO LOOK IN HERE FOR A BIT?

NOT ONLY DID GISELE LET HIM RANT AT HER ABOUT WHATEVER BAND HE WAS INTO AT THAT MOMENT,

HE WASN'T ALWAYS A BAD SINGER, HIS VOICE JUST WENT TO SHIT IN THE LATE '70's

BUT SHE EVEN SEEMED INTERESTED WHEN HE TALKED ABOUT HOW STOP MAKING SENSE WAS FILMED,

THEY SHOT IT OVER THREE NIGHTS SO YOU WOULDN'T SEE ANY CAMERAS.

WOW.

OR HOW ROBBIE ROBERTSON RUINED BOTH THE LAST WALTZ AND THE BASEMENT TAPES.

AND HE ADDED SONGS THAT THEY MADE AS DEMOS BEHIND HIS BACK!

AFTERWARDS, MARTIN AND GISELE SPENT DAYS AND NIGHTS TEXTING EACH OTHER. SUMMER DAYS AND SUMMER NIGHTS.

When can you hang out again?

IN FACT, MARTIN WENT ON VACATION TO PRINCE EDWARD ISLAND WITH HIS FAMILY FOR A WEEK

AND SPENT THE ENTIRE TIME IN HIS ROOM TEXTING HER.

WE'RE GOING TO THE BEACH, MARTIN!

IT WAS DURING THIS TIME THAT GISELE TOLD HIM KATHERINE HAD MOVED ON

She's seeing other guys

AND THAT HE SHOULD ALSO FIND SOMEONE ELSE.

But, I'm sure there's someone out there for you.

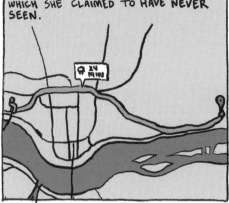

THAT'S PRETTY MUCH HOW, AFTER HE GOT HOME, MARTIN ENDED UP AT GISELE'S TO WATCH GHOSTBUSTERS, WHICH SHE CLAIMED TO HAVE NEVER SEEN.

I GUESS IT GOES WITHOUT SAYING THAT THEY DIDN'T SEE MUCH OF THE MOVIE.

YOU'RE GOING TO MISS THE FRIDGE!

I R

IT WAS IMMEDIATELY APPARENT THAT THERE WAS A SPARK BETWEEN THEM,

WHAT?

THAT THEY POSSESSED A MAGICAL SEXUAL ENERGY,

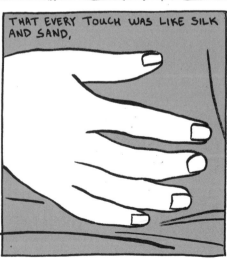

THAT EVERY TOUCH WAS LIKE SILK AND SAND,

AND THAT THEY INTUITIVELY KNEW WHAT THE OTHER WANTED.

TAKE OFF YOUR SHORTS

THAT FIRST AFTERNOON THEY SHARED THREE ORGASMS.

SHIT!

MARTIN CLAIMED THEY DID IT AN ABSURD AMOUNT OF TIMES DURING THOSE FIRST MONTHS,

STOPPING ONLY BRIEFLY WHEN HIS BLOOD SUGAR WOULD GET LOW.

I HAVE TO ADMIT I WAS SKEPTICAL AT FIRST ABOUT THE QUALITY OF THEIR SEX LIFE, BUT I ALSO ALWAYS SEEMED TO BE CATCHING THEM IN THE MIDDLE OF IT WHEN I WOULD COME TO INTERVIEW MARTIN.

HI

(UM)

SORRY TO KEEP YOU WAITING.

ANYWAY, THE NEXT TIME MARTIN SAW KATHERINE WAS A YEAR LATER AT GISELE'S PROM.

THEY ENDED UP SITTING AWKWARDLY BESIDE EACH OTHER, BARELY SAYING A WORD.

ON TOP OF HAVING A GREAT SEX LIFE, MARTIN AND GISELE HAVE A LOT GOING ON.

SO, ANY... WHEN SHE FIRST K...

HAVE YOU EVER SEEN ONE OF THOSE COUPLES WHO CLEARLY WERE MEANT TO BE,

UNNGH!

AND (UM)

WHO COMPLEMENT EACH OTHER BY MAKING UP FOR THE OTHER'S FLAWS,

#@^!

ONE SEC.

AND WHO ARE NEVER RESENTFUL OF EACH OTHERS SHORTCOMINGS?

YOU KNOW, THEY REALLY DON'T CONSIDER THE VERTICALLY CHALLENGED WHEN DESIGNING HOMES.

WELL, THAT'S THEM.

THANKS, BABE.

IT'S A SHAME THAT I HAD TO STOP SEEING THEM.

SORRY ABOUT THAT. WHERE WERE WE?

ONE OF THE MOST TOUCHING STORIES I EVER HEARD FROM THEM WAS GISELE'S DESCRIPTION OF THAT PARTY:

I WAS WITH MARTIN AND KATHERINE FOR MOST OF THE NIGHT.

"UNTIL THEY STARTED MAKING OUT,

"AND DISAPPEARED.

"THEN, AFTER MAYBE TEN, TWENTY MINUTES, KATHERINE REAPPEARED

WHERE'S MARTIN?

"AND TOLD ME MARTIN HAD PASSED OUT.

DOWNSTAIRS. WE WERE MAKING (UH) OUT AND HE PASSED OUT.

"SHE DIDN'T REALLY SEEM TO UNDERSTAND **HOW SERIOUS IT** CAN BE WHEN SOMEONE LIKE MARTIN PASSES OUT.

WHAT?

"APPARENTLY SHE DIDN'T KNOW HE WAS A DIABETIC. HOW THAT COULD BE IS BEYOND ME — EVERYONE AT F.H.S. SEEMED TO.

SHOULD I JUST GO AND LET HIM FIND HIS OWN WAY HOME?

"I TRIED TO GIVE HIM SOME SUGAR, BUT HE WAS OUT COLD.

MARTIN?

"SO, I CALLED 911

HI-I-UH-MY FRIEND IS-UH-HAS PASSED OUT AT A PARTY AND HE HAS-UM-DIE-DIABETES AND MY FATHER HAD IT TOO AND I KNOW IT'S BAD FOR HIM TO DRINK AND I CAN'T WAKE HIM, SO I DON'T KNOW WHAT TO DO—

"AND RODE WITH HIM TO THE HOSPITAL.

WELL, ONE OF US SHOULD!

"I WALKED HOME IN THE MORNING AND TOLD MY **MOM** I'D STAYED AT KATHERINE'S."

SO, I GUESS TO ANSWER THE WHOLE "WHERE ARE THEY NOW" QUESTION, MARTIN NOW LIVES IN MONCTON,

WITH HIS WIFE OF TWO YEARS

AND THEIR SIXTEEN-MONTH OLD DAUGHTER.

MARTIN CURRENTLY WORKS AS A "COACH" AT A CALL CENTRE

SO, WHAT COULD YOU HAVE DONE TO RESOLVE THIS CALL QUICKER?

AND GISELE IS A NURSE AT THE MONCTON HOSPITAL.

THEY PAID ME GOOD MONEY TO STAY IN THE PROVINCE. IT PAID OFF MY LOAN.

GIVEN THE RECENT ADVANCEMENTS IN TREATING DIABETES, I'LL CAUTIOUSLY END THIS BY SAYING "AND THEY LIVED HAPPILY EVER AFTER."

I WAS GOING TO END IT THERE. I REALIZED IT WOULD HAVE BEEN UNSATISFYING TO NOT TELL YOU ABOUT KATHERINE, BUT MARTIN NEVER GAVE ME HER REAL NAME, SO THERE REALLY WASN'T MUCH I COULD DO.

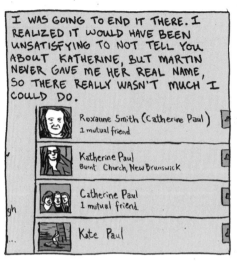

Roxanne Smith (Catherine Paul)
1 mutual friend

Katherine Paul
Burnt Church, New Brunswick

Catherine Paul
1 mutual friend

Kate Paul

BUT THEN, JUST AS I WAS FINISHING THIS ALL UP, I WAS AT ANOTHER ZINE FAIR IN FREDERICTON

patrickallaby

♡ ◯ ↱
♥ 25 Likes
patrickallaby I'm tabling today at FlowerF—

AND THIS WOMAN APPROACHED MY TABLE AND TOLD ME SHE WAS KATHERINE.

WELL, THAT'S NOT MY REAL NAME . . .

APPARENTLY, A FRIEND OF HERS WAS ONE OF THE THREE PEOPLE WHO BOUGHT PART 1 OFF OF ME THE LAST TIME I WAS IN FREDERICTON AND HAD LENT IT TO HER.

I READ YOUR COMIC ABOUT ME.

I'VE ALWAYS BEEN A BIT UNCOMFORTABLE AT THE PROSPECT OF SOMEONE RECOGNIZING THEMSELVES IN ONE OF MY COMICS AND NOT BEING AMUSED BY THEIR DEPICTION.

OH.

AND, WELL, "KATHERINE" WAS NOT AMUSED.

I LIKE YOUR DRAWINGS A LOT —

BUT READING IT MADE ME FEEL LIKE I WAS WATCHING A BAD MOVIE ADAPTATION OF MY LIFE.

BUT, YOU KNOW, SHE WAS THE ONLY PERSON WHO COULD FACT-CHECK MARTIN PETERS FOR ME. I WANTED TO KNOW WHAT SHE THOUGHT. SO, I GOT SOMEONE TO WATCH MY TABLE FOR ME AND WE WENT TO A NEARBY COFFEE SHOP TO TALK.

WE SAT THERE FOR WELL OVER AN HOUR AND SHE TOLD ME EVERYTHING I GOT WRONG, OR MISREPRESENTED.

WELL — AND I'M SORRY IF THIS COMES ACROSS AS A BIT HARSH.

SHE THOUGHT I DOWNPLAYED HOW MUCH MARTIN LOVED THE SOUND OF HIS OWN VOICE,

BUT THEN AGAIN, IT'S NOT LIKE POST-WATERS FLOYD WAS WORSE MUSICALLY, JUST LYRICALLY. AND THAT'S WHAT I MEAN! THERE'S [RE]ALLY NO POSITION I TAKE WITHOUT —

AND THAT I'D FAILED TO CAPTURE HOW OVERTLY RACIST HE'D BEEN.

ARE THE DRUGS REALLY BAD ON YOUR REZ?

SHE ALSO MENTIONED THAT MARTIN HAD DISPLAYED SO LITTLE INTEREST IN HER PHYSICALLY WHEN THEY FIRST DATED THAT SHE THOUGHT HE WAS GAY.

APPARENTLY, THEY WOULD EVEN HAVE CONVERSATIONS ABOUT TRYING TO JUDGE THE SIZE OF TEACHERS' PENISES THROUGH THEIR PANTS.

SOMETIMES, I GET SO DISTRACTED BY IT THAT I TOTALLY ZONE OUT FOR THE REST OF CLASS.

"KATHERINE" ALSO TALKED A LOT ABOUT HOW THE SECOND TIME THEY DATED, SHE FELT LIKE MARTIN WAS JUST USING HER FOR WEED,

MAYBE WE SHOULD SMOKE ANOTHER BOWL?

um

NEVER ONCE HAVING CONTRIBUTED ANY, OR EVEN BOTHERING TO BUY HER A NEW PIPE.

PERHAPS WORST OF ALL, THOUGH, WAS THAT I DIDN'T EVEN ATTEMPT TO CAPTURE HOW CRUEL HIDING HIS DIABETES WAS,

YOU MADE IT SEEM LIKE HE ENDED UP IN THE E.R. BECAUSE I WAS TOO STONED TO NOTICE WHAT WAS GOING ON.

HOW IT MADE HER COME ACROSS AS A HEARTLESS BITCH.

WHEN, IN FACT HE COULD HAVE DIED BECAUSE HE DIDN'T TRUST ME! DIDN'T RESPECT ME.

BY THE TIME I GOT BACK TO THE ZINE FAIR, EVERYONE HAD PACKED UP.

THANKS

THIS BOOK WOULD NOT HAVE BEEN POSSIBLE WITHOUT THE FRIENDSHIP AND SUPPORT OF ANDY BROWN, ARTSNB, GEORDIE+ JESKA, STEVEN LAMBKE, GABRIELLE BELL, JOAN+ STEPHEN, MONICA, JONATHAN ROTSZTAIN, KAREN SNEIDER, NELLY, KRISTA, RACHEL, TODD, SAPPYFEST, STRUTS, STEVE HALEY, JON MCKIEL, SAVANNAH, JEFF, KEVIN, JORDYN+ KYLE, LAUREN, PAULA, ZAHRA, AND LIKE A HUNDRED OTHER PEOPLE (INCLUDING, BUT NOT LIMITED TO JOHN+GEMEY, SHARY, EVAN, MEGHAN, THE OWENS, KLARKA, AMANDA, RYAN, JERRY, GRAEME, OLIVIA, THE WATSONS+NIK, THUNDER+LIGHTNING, BOB DYLAN, LOU REED, PATTI SMITH, M.I.A., LIDO PIMIENTA, BANTING+BESS, LAURIE ANDERSON, AND MR. STONE). PAUL MARTIN, KATHERINE BUSH, AND PETER MANSBRIDGE ALSO DESERVE TO BE THANKED. SO DOES LAURA. I DON'T KNOW WHAT I'D DO WITHOUT YOU. THANKS FOR YOUR PATIENCE AS I HAVE FIGURED OUT HOW TO DO THIS. I'D ALSO LIKE TO THANK YOU. THANK YOU SO MUCH FOR TAKING THE TIME TO READ. I HOPE YOU DIDN'T HATE IT, AND DIDN'T FIND IT OBJECTIONABLE. I REALLY DID TRY.

PATRICK ALLABY

WAS BORN ON AUGUST 21, 1993 AT THE CHALMER'S HOSPITAL IN FREDERICTON, NEW BRUNSWICK WITH FOUR THUMBS. HIS EXTRA THUMBS WERE REMOVED THAT FALL, AND HE HAS NOT BEEN ABLE TO BEND HIS THUMBS EVER SINCE. HIS NEXT MEDICAL PROCEDURE WAS IN JANUARY 2003. HE WAS CIRCUMCISED. HE BROKE HIS ARM IN MAY 2006 WHILE BIKING NEAR HIS HOUSE. HE HAD A CAST ON HIS LEFT ARM FOR SIX WEEKS. HE SUFFERED A CONCUSSION WHILE PLAYING COMPETITIVE HOCKEY IN DECEMBER, 2008. HE WAS HOSPITALIZED FOR ALCOHOL POISONING, WHILE WORKING ON A PERFORMANCE ART PIECE, ON MARCH 16, 2012. THE NEXT TIME HE WAS HOSPITALIZED WAS IN DECEMBER, 2015. DURING THIS VISIT, HE WAS DIAGNOSED WITH TYPE 1 DIABETES.